Magpies,

Homebodies,

AND

NOMADS

A MODERN KNITTER'S GUIDE TO DISCOVERING AND EXPLORING STYLE

CIRILIA ROSE

PHOTOGRAPHY BY JARED FLOOD

STC CRAFT | A MELANIE FALICK BOOK   NEW YORK

Published in 2014 by Stewart, Tabori & Chang
An imprint of ABRAMS

Library of Congress Control Number: 2014930829

ISBN: 978-1-58479-953-5

Editor: Melanie Falick
Designer: Deb Wood
Production Manager: Denise LaCongo

The text of this book was composed in Futura and Garamond

Printed and bound in China

10 9 8 7 6 5 4 3 2 1

ABRAMS
THE ART OF BOOKS SINCE 1949

115 West 18th Street
New York, NY 10011
www.abramsbooks.com

FINDING YOUR INNER BRICOLEUR

MODERN KNITTERS ARE MYRIAD.

They defy definition, occupying so many sorts of bodies, beliefs, and lifestyles that to attempt to describe the "average knitter" would be something of a fool's game. Yet there is still a word that applies to most knitters—an action every knitter engages in daily, hourly, moment to moment, from their yarn shops to their dorm rooms to their urban homesteads. All of these knitters are rampant bricoleurs.

I first came across the term "bricolage" in a university classroom, where I was assigned to read *Subculture: The Meaning of Style* by Dick Hebdige, a British sociologist. I was floored to learn that the study of style existed and even more floored to learn that Hebdige seemed to describe something I was observing everywhere. Writing 21 years before the turn of the millennium, he hinted that the only way left to achieve originality was through the mixture of cultural referents. I agreed, and I later came to realize that this is a theory uniquely suited to modern knitters and knitwear designers.

The past decade has seen a proliferation of knitwear designers, myself included, and we're all working from essentially the same sourcebooks, with the same basic resources: the knit stitch, the purl stitch, and a whole lot of yarn. So how does one innovate in an increasingly crowded landscape? The answer is, of course, through bricolage. The combination of elements from seemingly disparate cultural sources creates energy that didn't exist before, and when each of us cultivates our own unique concoction of referents, it guarantees more idiosyncratic knits.

Even if you don't consider yourself a designer, you probably put a lot of thought and effort into each project. I've joked that this is my favorite part of the process, something that I honed during years of working in a busy yarn store in the Northeast, helping thousands of knitters in the initial planning stages of their projects. The thought and care that go into choosing a pattern, a yarn, a color scheme, and even a size are enormous harbingers of a project's success. They can make the difference between the schlumpy, ill-fitting sweater that we've seen in countless clueless sitcoms and a couture-quality garment that you can get downright smug about.

I've divided the projects in this book into three sections that I feel are three parts of a knitterly personality. We're all Magpies, collecting small amounts of precious yarns and never knowing quite what to do with them. We're Homebodies, sometimes preferring the quiet of our own perch, but we're also Nomads, venturing into the world to meet friends and gather inspiration. At the end of each chapter I have included Style Inspiration entries in which I share my own thoughts on the design process and how I wear and style handknits. I hope these essays will help you learn how to think like a designer, which can make a huge difference in your knitting and your personal style.

People often ask me how I became a knitwear designer, and I tell them that I have to come to terms with the title daily. Acknowledging your own style and then your creative faculties requires work, but your yarn, needles, and the contents of your closets can become your atelier.

LET'S GET GOING...

FOR THOSE SMALL AMOUNTS OF PRECIOUS YARNS WE INEVITABLY COLLECT

Magpies

I AM, AS I SUSPECT MANY OF YOU ARE, ADDICTED TO YARN.

Knitters are exceptional collectors, and we have intricate relationships with our respective collections. I realized at some point that the enjoyment I get from planning projects and acquiring the supplies to complete them is almost as fulfilling as the back end of that process. This served me well when I worked at a yarn store where my main task was to assist customers with the planning and execution of projects. A fellow yarn shop employee christened us with a wonderful title—creative consultants. We provided assurance, inspiration, and guidance, and we delighted in the vicarious shopping experience.

My own yarn-shopping habits are unique and universal at the same time. Many of my colleagues report that they no longer purchase yarn, and really, why should they? Between the discounts and the samples that tend to accumulate, we all have or have access to more than enough fiber to complete any project. And yet I find myself still feeling the familiar magpie twitch when faced with a gorgeous skein. Without need or intention, I buy it and add it to the family. Without a plan, these skeins are full of pure kinetic energy, frightening and thrilling at the same time.

These new additions are rarely practical. They're often gorgeous and luxurious, and without a project in mind it's difficult for me to justify buying more than one or two skeins. They often hold sentimental value, and terroir, serving as a portal back to a treasured place and time. These unplanned adoptions are highly emotional, which means they are generally exceptional in some way. It could be a rare fiber that I have never worked with, or a masterfully rendered hand-painted version of a favorite color. It could be pure novelty, something that I don't think I'll ever come across again, or a long-discontinued favorite hidden away undiscovered on a quiet shelf.

Because of this, the single skein stash forms a particularly telling backlog. When I rifle through these oddments, I travel through phases and whims from my past. I love to see scrap projects that people make from their own oddballs. They're always curiously harmonious, and of course they are—even the most wildly fickle knitters have a core palette that they remain true to. There tends to be a noticeable throughline, which makes it easy to incorporate these vintage skeins into current projects.

Combining two seemingly disparate yarns can result in a striking cowl like Breve, a study in contrasts that also extends the life of two small skeins. Adding unique fibers like shiny mohair locks to an otherwise basic cardigan can elevate the piece and serve as a standalone accessory like the Marion Collar. The magpie impulse often extends beyond yarn, as seen with the Norah Hat. Vintage patches or buttons are all too easy to add to the amorphous collection, and they're such fun starting points. I knew that the navy blue sequined patch from the 1940s deserved to take center stage. Placing it on a small cloche meant it would be the focal point, especially when worn dramatically cocked to one side. I do this sort of inverse designing all the time, which makes it all too easy to justify expanding my collection of notions, hardware, and embellishments. I never know what will form around a particularly lovely trinket or what a tiny bit of yarn will spark. Use it for embroidery or a piped cast-on or bind-off row—a contrast-color hint of silk at the edge of a mohair cardigan is exactly the sort of detail store-bought sweaters rarely have. Whatever their final use, treasure these impractical skeins because they hold an inordinate amount of knitterly magic.

NORAH HAT

Embellishment, trim, hardware, notions, bric-a-brac—whatever you call it, I'm obsessed with finishing details. The irony is, my designs often start with the tiny pieces I find in haberdasheries around the world and online. Rather than buy buttons, hooks, or snaps as an afterthought, I stockpile these items and will often design around them. The vintage sequin patch shown here was a souvenir from an incredible independent fabric store in Columbia, South Carolina. It serves as a portal for daydreaming: remembering the time I spent browsing with a friend, and wondering who owned the patch before, what it might have adorned, and where it might have been worn.

    The woven cable brim of Norah is knit first, subtly shaped with needle size changes. The remainder is picked up and knit, and the patch is added last, straddling the ornate brim and simpler stockinette cap for an organic, decoupaged feel.

SIZES
Small (Medium, Large)

FINISHED MEASUREMENTS
16¾ (19¼, 21½)" [42.5 (49, 54.5) cm] circumference

Note: Hat is supposed to fit snugly.

YARN
HiKoo Kenzie [50% New Zealand merino / 25% nylon / 10% angora / 10% alpaca / 5% silk noils; 160 yards (146.5 meters) / 50 grams]: 2 skeins #1009 Oceania

NEEDLES
One 16" (40 cm) long circular (circ) needle size US 6 (4 mm)

One set of five double-pointed needles (dpn) size US 6 (4 mm)

One pair straight needles size US 7 (4.5 mm)

One pair straight needles size US 8 (5 mm)

Change needle size if necessary to obtain correct gauge.

NOTIONS
Crochet hook size US G/6 (4 mm); waste yarn; cable needle; stitch markers; sequined patch approx 5" (12.5 cm) wide at widest point; tapestry needle (if working Kitchener st); sewing needle and thread

GAUGE
20 sts and 28 rows = 4" (10 cm) in Stockinette stitch (St st), using size US 6 (4 mm) needles

ABBREVIATIONS
C8B: Slip 4 sts to cable needle, hold to back, k4, k4 from cable needle.

C8F: Slip 4 sts to cable needle, hold to front, k4, k4 from cable needle.

NOTE
If you are unsure which size to work, try Band on as you go; work until it fits your head snugly, but comfortably, ending with Row 12 of Woven Cable and making sure that you have an even number of vertical repeats of Woven Cable. Then for the Body, pick up 1 st per ridge as instructed, and based on the number of sts you picked up, work that size for the remainder of the pattern.

STITCH PATTERN

Woven Cable

(panel of 28 sts; 12-row repeat)

ROW 1 AND ALL WS ROWS: K2, purl to last 2 sts, k2.

ROWS 2 AND 4: Knit.

ROW 6: K2, [C8F] 3 times, k2.

ROWS 8 AND 10: Knit.

ROW 12: K6, [C8B] twice, k6.

Repeat Rows 1–12 for *Woven Cable*.

BAND

Using crochet hook, waste yarn, and Provisional (Crochet Chain) CO (see Special Techniques, page 142), CO 28 sts. Change to size US 6 (4 mm) dpns and working yarn. Purl 1 row. Begin Woven Cable; work Rows 1–12 twice.

Change to size US 7 (4.5 mm) needles; work Rows 1–12 twice.

Change to size US 8 (5 mm) needles; work Rows 1–12 six (8, 10) times.

Change to size US 7 (4.5 mm) needles; work Rows 1–12 twice.

Change to size US 6 (4 mm) needles; work Rows 1–12 twice. Purl 1 row. Cut yarn, leaving an 18" (45.5 cm) tail. Transfer sts to waste yarn.

BODY

With RS of Band facing, using circ needle, pick up and knit 84 (96, 108) sts along long side edge of Band, picking up 1 st in each ridge along edge. Join for working in the rnd; pm for beginning of rnd. Begin St st; work even until piece measures 2½" (6.5 cm) from pick-up rnd, placing marker every 7 (8, 9) sts on last rnd.

SHAPE CROWN

NOTE: *Change to size US 6 (4 mm) dpns when necessary for number of sts on needle.*

DECREASE RND: Decrease 12 sts this rnd, then every other rnd 5 (6, 7) times, as follows: *Knit to 2 sts before marker, k2tog; repeat from * to end—12 sts remain.

Cut yarn, leaving a 12" (30.5 cm) tail. Thread tail through sts twice, pull tight, and fasten off.

FINISHING

With RS facing, carefully unravel Provisional CO and place sts on an empty size US 6 (4 mm) dpn. Transfer sts from waste yarn to empty size US 6 (4 mm) dpn. Using Three-Needle BO or Kitchener st (see Special Techniques, page 141), graft ends of Band together.

Block as desired. Using sewing needle and thread, sew on sequined patch (see photo).

BREVE COWL

The simple lace stitch forms a stretchy net of intersecting diagonal lines and a slipped-stitch edge looks neat and encourages a graceful drape. Rowan Denim yarn slowly fades with each wash, just as real dungarees do. The gently shifting shades of Noro Silk Garden resemble a favorite plaid shirt, worn and comfortable, with unexpected color combinations. If you substitute a lighter shade of yarn, be sure to wash the denim portion before joining the second yarn to test for colorfastness, as the indigo-dyed Denim can bleed.

FINISHED MEASUREMENTS
7" (18 cm) wide x 56" (142 cm) circumference

YARN
Rowan Denim [100% cotton; 100 yards (91.5 meters) / 50 grams]: 1 skein #225 Nashville (A)

Noro Silk Garden [45% silk / 45% mohair / 10% lambswool; 110 yards (100.5 meters) / 50 grams]: 1 skein #349 (B)

NEEDLES
One pair straight needles size US 9 (5.5 mm)

Change needle size if necessary to obtain correct gauge.

NOTIONS
Crochet hook size US J/10 (6 mm); waste yarn; tapestry needle (if working Kitchener st)

GAUGE
12 sts and 18 rows = 4" (10 cm) in Biasing Lace

Note: Gauge is not critical for this project.

STITCH PATTERN
Biasing Lace
(multiple of 2 sts + 7; 2-row repeat)
ROW 1 (RS): Slip 3 wyib, k1, *yo, k2tog; repeat from * to last 3 sts, k3.
ROW 2: Slip 3 wyib, purl to end.
Repeat Rows 1 and 2 for *Biasing Lace.*

COWL

Using crochet hook, waste yarn and Provisional (Crochet Chain) CO (see Special Techniques, page 142), CO 29 sts. Change to A. Purl 1 row. Begin Biasing Lace; work even until yarn is used up, ending at side edge. Change to B; work even until you have approximately 24" (61 cm) of yarn left, ending with Row 2 of pattern.

FINISHING

With RS facing, carefully unravel Provisional CO and place sts on empty needle. Using Three-Needle BO or Kitchener st (see Special Techniques, page 141), graft ends of Cowl together. Block well, making sure to stretch side edges.

FRAMBOISE CARDIGAN + SCARF

Style advisors love to sing the praises of silk scarves. The fluid fabric and the idiosyncratic prints make them highly collectible items, but I often find myself cursing the magazine editors who claim that they're an easy, transformative item. The slinky fabric can be difficult to manage, and intricate ties can end up feeling overly fussy. Framboise is a simple, ladylike cardigan with two petite tabs that will hold a favorite scarf in place. Knit the challenging lace ascot (shown here in a non-slippery silk-wool blend) or substitute a treasured vintage piece.

FRAMBOISE CARDIGAN

SIZES
To fit bust sizes 31 (33, 35, 37, 39, 41, 45, 49, 53)" [78.5 (84, 89, 94, 99, 104, 114.5, 124.5, 134.5) cm]

FINISHED MEASUREMENTS
33 (35, 37, 39, 41, 43, 47, 51, 55)" [84 (89, 94, 99, 104, 108, 119.5, 129.5, 139.5) cm] bust, buttoned

YARN
Manos del Uruguay Silk Blend [70% merino wool / 30% silk; 150 yards (137 meters) / 50 grams]: 7 (7, 8, 8, 8, 9, 10, 10, 11) hanks #300G Coffee

NEEDLES
One pair straight needles size US 5 (3.75 mm)

One pair straight needles size US 6 (4 mm)

One 40" (100 cm) long circular (circ) needle size US 5 (3.75 mm)

Change needle size if necessary to obtain correct gauge.

NOTIONS
Waste yarn or stitch holder; stitch markers; nine ¾" (19 mm) buttons

GAUGE
20 sts and 28 rows = 4" (10 cm) in Stockinette stitch (St st), using larger needles

STITCH PATTERN
Twisted Rib
(even number of sts; 2-row repeat)
ROW 1 (RS): *K1-tbl, p1; repeat from * to end, end k1-tbl if working over an odd number of sts.
ROW 2: Purl the purl sts tbl and knit the knit sts as they face you. Repeat Rows 1 and 2 for *Twisted Rib*.

SPECIAL TECHNIQUE
ONE-ROW BUTTONHOLE: Slip 1 wyif, bring yarn to back and leave it there (you won't use it while you are slipping sts), slip 1 wyib, pass first slipped st over second slipped st; [slip 1 wyib, pass slipped st over] 3 times; slip last slipped st back to left-hand needle, turn. Bring yarn to back; using Cable Cast-On Method (see Special Techniques, page 141), CO 5 sts, turn; wyib, slip 1 st from left-hand needle back to right-hand needle; pass last CO st over slipped st. Continue with row.

BACK

Using smaller straight needles, CO 79 (85, 89, 95, 99, 105, 115, 125, 135) sts. Begin Twisted Rib; work even for 1" (2.5 cm), ending with a WS row.

NEXT ROW (RS): Change to larger needles and St st; work even until piece measures 3½" (7.5 cm) from the beginning, increasing 1 (0, 1, 0, 1, 0, 0, 0, 0) st(s) on first row, and ending with a WS row—80 (85, 90, 95, 100, 105, 115, 125, 135) sts.

SHAPE WAIST

NEXT ROW (RS): Decrease 1 st each side this row, then every 6 rows 4 times, as follows: K2, ssk, knit to last 4 sts, k2tog, k2—70 (75, 80, 85, 90, 95, 105, 115, 125) sts remain. Work even for 7 rows.

SHAPE BUST

NEXT ROW (RS): Increase 1 st each side this row, then every 6 rows 4 times, as follows: K2, M1-r, knit to last 2 sts, M1-l, k2—80 (85, 90, 95, 100, 105, 115, 125, 135) sts. Work even until back measures 12½" (32 cm) from the beginning, ending with a WS row.

SHAPE ARMHOLES

NEXT ROW (RS): BO 5 (5, 6, 6, 7, 8, 10, 11, 13) sts at beginning of next two rows, 2 sts at beginning of next 0 (0, 0, 0, 2, 2, 4, 6, 8) rows, then decrease 1 st each side every 4 rows 3 (4, 4, 5, 4, 5, 4, 4, 4) times, as follows: K2, ssk, knit to last 4 sts, k2tog, k2—64 (67, 70, 73, 74, 75, 79, 83, 85) sts remain. Work even until armholes measure 7 (7½, 7½, 8, 8, 8¼, 8½, 8¾, 9)" [18 (19, 19, 20.5, 20.5, 21, 21.5, 22, 23) cm], ending with a WS row.

SHAPE NECK AND SHOULDERS

NEXT ROW (RS): K17 (18, 19, 20, 20, 20, 21, 23, 24), join a second ball of yarn, BO center 30 (31, 32, 33, 34, 35, 37, 37, 37) sts, knit to end. Working both sides at the same time, BO 4 (5, 5, 5, 5, 5, 5, 6, 6) sts at beginning of next 6 rows, then 5 (3, 4, 5, 5, 5, 6, 5, 6) sts at beginning of next 2 rows.

RIGHT FRONT

Using smaller straight needles, CO 40 (42, 44, 48, 50, 52, 58, 62, 68) sts. Begin Twisted Rib; work even for 1" (2.5 cm), ending with a WS row.

NEXT ROW (RS): Change to larger needles and St st; work even until piece measures 3½" (7.5 cm) from the beginning, increasing 0 (1, 1, 0, 0, 0, 0, 0, 0) st(s) on first row, and ending with a WS row—40 (43, 45, 48, 50, 52, 58, 62, 68) sts.

SHAPE WAIST

NEXT ROW (RS): Decrease 1 st this row, then every 6 rows 4 times, as follows: Knit to last 4 sts, k2tog, k2—35 (38, 40, 43, 45, 47, 53, 57, 63) sts remain. Work even for 7 rows.

SHAPE BUST

NEXT ROW (RS): Increase 1 st this row, then every 6 rows 4 times, as follows: Knit to last 2 sts, M1-l, k2—40 (43, 45, 48, 50, 52, 58, 62, 68) sts. Work even until piece measures 12½" (32 cm) from the beginning, ending with a RS row.

SHAPE ARMHOLE AND NECK

NOTE: *Armhole and neck are shaped at the same time; please read entire section through before beginning.*

NEXT ROW (WS): BO 5 (5, 6, 6, 7, 8, 10, 11, 13) sts at armhole edge once, then 2 sts 0 (0, 0, 0, 1, 1, 2, 3, 4) time(s), then decrease 1 st at armhole edge every 4 rows 3 (4, 4, 5, 4, 5, 4, 4, 4) times, as follows: Work to last 4 sts, k2tog, k2. AT THE SAME TIME, beginning on first RS row of armhole shaping, begin neck shaping as follows:

NEXT ROW (RS): Decrease 1 st at neck edge this row, every other row 5 (5, 5, 6, 6, 5, 9, 6, 8) times, then every 4 rows 9 (10, 10, 10, 10, 11, 9, 11, 10) times, as follows: Ssk, work to end—17 (18, 19, 20, 20, 20, 21, 23, 24) sts remain when all shaping is complete. Work even until armhole measures 7 (7½, 7½, 8, 8, 8¼, 8½, 8¾, 9)" [18 (19, 19, 20.5, 20.5, 21, 21.5, 22, 23) cm], ending with a RS row.

SHAPE SHOULDER

NEXT ROW (WS): BO 4 (5, 5, 5, 5, 5, 5, 6, 6) sts at armhole edge 3 times, then 5 (3, 4, 5, 5, 5, 6, 5, 6) sts once.

LEFT FRONT

Using smaller straight needles, CO 40 (42, 44, 48, 50, 52, 58, 62, 68) sts. Begin Twisted Rib, beginning with a purl st; work even for 1" (2.5 cm), ending with a WS row.

NEXT ROW (RS): Change to larger needles and St st; work even until piece measures 3½" (7.5 cm) from the beginning, increasing 0 (1, 1, 0, 0, 0, 0, 0, 0) st(s) on first row, and ending with a WS row—40 (43, 45, 48, 50, 52, 58, 62, 68) sts.

SHAPE WAIST

NEXT ROW (RS): Decrease 1 st this row, then every 6 rows 4 times, as follows: K2, ssk, knit to end—35 (38, 40, 43, 45, 47, 53, 57, 63) sts remain. Work even for 7 rows.

SHAPE BUST

NEXT ROW (RS): Increase 1 st this row, then every 6 rows 4 times, as follows: K2, M1-r, knit to end—40 (43, 45, 48, 50, 52, 58, 62, 68) sts. Work even until piece measures 12½" (32 cm) from the beginning, ending with a WS row.

SHAPE ARMHOLE AND NECK

NOTE: *Armhole and neck are shaped at the same time; please read entire section through before beginning.*

NEXT ROW (RS): BO 5 (5, 6, 6, 7, 8, 10, 11, 13) sts at armhole edge once, then 2 sts 0 (0, 0, 0, 1, 1, 2, 3, 4) time(s), then decrease 1 st at armhole edge every 4 rows 3 (4, 4, 5, 4, 5, 4, 4, 4) times, as follows: K2, ssk, work to end. AT THE SAME TIME, beginning on first RS row of armhole shaping, begin neck shaping as follows:

NEXT ROW (RS): Decrease 1 st at neck edge this row, every other row 5 (5, 5, 6, 6, 5, 9, 6, 8) times, then every 4 rows 9 (10, 10, 10, 10, 11, 9, 11, 10) times, as follows: Work to last 2 sts, k2tog—17 (18, 19, 20, 20, 20, 21, 23, 24) sts remain when all shaping is complete. Work even until armhole measures 7 (7½, 7½, 8, 8, 8¼, 8½, 8¾, 9)" [18 (19, 19, 20.5, 20.5, 21, 21.5, 22, 23) cm], ending with a WS row.

SHAPE SHOULDER

NEXT ROW (RS): BO 4 (5, 5, 5, 5, 5, 5, 6, 6) sts at armhole edge 3 times, then 5 (3, 4, 5, 5, 5, 6, 5, 6) sts once.

SLEEVES

Using smaller straight needles, CO 44 (44, 46, 48, 50, 50, 56, 58, 62) sts. Begin Twisted Rib; work even for 1" (2.5 cm), ending with a WS row.

NEXT ROW (RS): Change to larger needles and St st; work even for 2 rows, increase 1 st on first row—45 (45, 47, 49, 51, 51, 57, 59, 63) sts.

SHAPE SLEEVE

NEXT ROW (RS): Increase 1 st each side this row, every other row 0 (3, 5, 7, 9, 11, 11, 13, 14) times, then every 4 rows 5 (4, 3, 2, 1, 0, 0, 0, 0) time(s), working increased sts in St st as they become available, as follows: K1, M1-r, knit to last st, M1-l —57 (61, 65, 69, 73, 75, 81, 87, 93) sts. Work even until piece measures 6" (15 cm) from the beginning, ending with a WS row.

SHAPE CAP

NEXT ROW (RS): BO 5 (5, 6, 6, 7, 8, 10, 11, 13) sts at beginning of next 2 rows, decrease 1 st each side every other row 10 (13, 14, 15, 16, 16, 15, 17, 18) times, then every 4 rows 1 (0, 0, 0, 0, 0, 1, 1, 1) time(s), then BO 4 sts at beginning of next 4 rows. BO remaining 9 (9, 9, 11, 11, 11, 13, 13, 13) sts.

FINISHING

Block as desired. Sew shoulder seams. Set in Sleeves. Sew side and Sleeve seams.

NECKBAND

Using smaller circular needle, beginning at lower Right Front edge, pick up and knit approximately 2 sts for every 3 rows, and 1 st for each BO st around neck edge to lower Left Front edge, ending with an odd number of sts. Begin Twisted Rib; work even for 3 rows. Place markers for 7 buttonholes on Right Front, the first ½" (1.5 cm) up from lower edge, the last at beginning of neck shaping, and the remaining 5 evenly spaced between.

BUTTONHOLE ROW: [Work to marker, work One-Row Buttonhole] 7 times, work to end. Work even for 4 rows. BO all sts in rib. Sew 7 buttons to Left Front, opposite buttonholes.

SCARF TABS (MAKE 2)

With WS facing, using smaller needles, and beginning just above top button or buttonhole, pick up and knit 6 sts in edge of Neckband. **NOTE:** *The Tabs will be folded over to the RS of each Front, so that the purl side of the Tab will be facing the RS of the Front.* In the following rows, "RS" refers to the knit side of the Tab, which will be visible when the Tab is buttoned to the Front. Begin St st, beginning with a WS (purl) row; work even for 2" (5 cm), ending with a WS row.

SHAPE TAB

ROW 1 (RS): K3, yo, k2tog, k1.

ROWS 2 AND 4: Purl.

ROW 3: K1, ssk, k2tog, k1—4 sts remain.

ROW 5: Ssk, k2tog—2 sts remain.

ROW 6: P2tog—1 st remains. Fasten off.

Fold Scarf Tabs so that WS of Tab is facing RS of Front; sew 2 buttons to Fronts, opposite buttonholes.

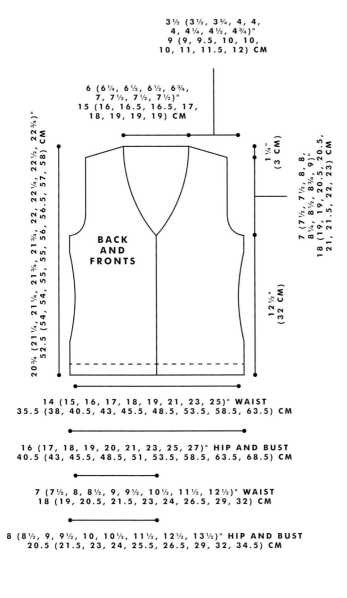

3 ½ (3 ½, 3 ¾, 4, 4, 4, 4 ¼, 4 ½, 4 ¾)"
9 (9, 9.5, 10, 10, 10, 11, 11.5, 12) CM

6 (6 ¼, 6 ½, 6 ½, 6 ¾, 7, 7 ½, 7 ½, 7 ½)"
15 (16, 16.5, 16.5, 17, 18, 19, 19, 19) CM

1 ¼" (3 CM)

7 (7 ½, 7 ½, 8, 8, 8 ¼, 8 ½, 8 ¾, 9)"
18 (19, 19, 20.5, 20.5, 21, 21.5, 22, 23) CM

20 ¾ (21 ¼, 21 ¼, 21 ¾, 22, 22 ¼, 22 ½, 22 ¾)"
52.5 (54, 54, 55, 56, 56.5, 57, 58) CM

BACK AND FRONTS

12 ½" (32 CM)

14 (15, 16, 17, 18, 19, 21, 23, 25)" WAIST
35.5 (38, 40.5, 43, 45.5, 48.5, 53.5, 58.5, 63.5) CM

16 (17, 18, 19, 20, 21, 23, 25, 27)" HIP AND BUST
40.5 (43, 45.5, 48.5, 51, 53.5, 58.5, 63.5, 68.5) CM

7 (7 ½, 8, 8 ½, 9, 9 ½, 10 ½, 11 ½, 12 ½)" WAIST
18 (19, 20.5, 21.5, 23, 24, 26.5, 29, 32) CM

8 (8 ½, 9, 9 ½, 10, 10 ½, 11 ½, 12 ½, 13 ½)" HIP AND BUST
20.5 (21.5, 23, 24, 25.5, 26.5, 29, 32, 34.5) CM

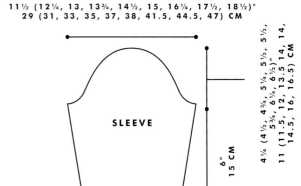

11 ½ (12 ¼, 13, 13 ¾, 14 ½, 15, 16 ¼, 17 ½, 18 ½)"
29 (31, 33, 35, 37, 38, 41.5, 44.5, 47) CM

4 ¼ (4 ½, 4 ¾, 5 ¼, 5 ½, 5 ½, 5 ¾, 6 ¼, 6 ½)"
11 (11.5, 12, 13.5, 14, 14.5, 16, 16.5) CM

SLEEVE

6" 15 CM

9 (9, 9 ½, 9 ¾, 10 ¼, 10 ¼, 11 ½, 11 ¾, 12 ½)"
23 (23, 24, 25, 26, 26, 29, 30, 32) CM

FRAMBOISE SCARF

FINISHED MEASUREMENTS
Approximately 10½" (26.5 cm) wide at widest point x 50" (127 cm) long

YARN
Manos del Uruguay Silk Blend [70% merino wool / 30% silk; 150 yards (137 meters) / 50 grams]: 2 hanks #300S Magenta.

NEEDLES
One pair straight needles size US 7 (4.5 mm)

One pair straight needles size US 8 (5 mm)

One pair straight needles size US 9 (5.5 mm)

One pair straight needles size US 10 (6 mm)

Change needle size if necessary to obtain correct gauge.

NOTIONS
Crochet hook size US H/8 (5 mm); waste yarn

GAUGE
20 sts and 28 rows = 4" (10 cm) in Stockinette stitch (St st), using size US 7 (4.5 mm) needles

14 sts and 20 rows = 4" (10 cm) in Lace Ribbon Stitch, using size US 10 (6 mm) needles

NOTE
The Scarf begins with a Provisional Cast-On and is worked in two Sections. The First Section is worked in Lace Ribbon Stitch to the bind-off edge. The Second Section is picked up from the Provisional Cast-On and worked in the opposite direction, beginning with short-row shaping in Stockinette stitch to shape the Scarf across the back neck, and ending with Lace Ribbon Stitch as for the First Section.

STITCH PATTERN

Lace Ribbon Stitch (see Chart) (multiple of 10 sts + 7; 12-row repeat)

NOTE: *Slip all sts purlwise.*

ROW 1 (RS): Slip 1, k1, *ssk, yo, k5, k2tog, yo, k1; repeat from * to last 5 sts, ssk, yo, k3.

ROW 2: Slip 1, p1, *p2tog, yo, p2, yo, p1, p2tog, p3; repeat from * to last 5 sts, p2tog, yo, p3.

ROW 3: Slip 1, k1, *ssk, yo, k3, k2tog, k2, yo, k1; repeat from * to last 5 sts, ssk, yo, k3.

ROW 4: Slip 1, p1, *p2tog, yo, p2, yo, p3, p2tog, p1; repeat from * to last 5 sts, p2tog, yo, p3.

ROW 5: Slip 1, k1, *ssk, yo, k2, ssk, k3, yo, k1; repeat from * to last 5 sts, ssk, yo, k3.

ROW 6: Slip 1, p1, *p2tog, yo, p2, yo, p3, p2tog-tbl, p1; repeat from * to last 5 sts, p2tog, yo, p3.

ROW 7: Slip 1, k1, *ssk, yo, k2, yo, ssk, k4; repeat from * to last 5 sts, ssk, yo, k3.

ROW 8: Slip 1, p1, *p2tog, yo, p4, p2tog-tbl, p1, yo, p1; repeat from * to last 5 sts, p2tog, yo, p3.

ROW 9: Slip 1, k1, *ssk, [yo, k2] twice, ssk, k2; repeat from * to last 5 sts, ssk, yo, k3.

ROW 10: Slip 1, p1, *p2tog, yo, p2, p2tog-tbl, p3, yo, p1; repeat from * to last 5 sts, p2tog, yo, p3.

ROW 11: Slip 1, k1, *ssk, yo, k2, yo, k3, k2tog, k1; repeat from * to last 5 sts, ssk, yo, k3.

ROW 12: Slip 1, p1, *p2tog, yo, p2, p2tog, p3, yo, p1; repeat from * to last 5 sts, p2tog, yo, p3.

Repeat Rows 1–12 for *Lace Ribbon Stitch*.

SPECIAL TECHNIQUE

SPECIAL TECHNIQUE

PICOT BIND-OFF: BO 1 st, slip st back to left-hand needle, *CO 2 sts using Cable CO (see Special Techniques, page 141), BO 3 sts, slip st back to left-hand needle; repeat from * until all sts have been BO.

FIRST SECTION

Using crochet hook, waste yarn, and Provisional (Crochet Chain) CO (see Special Techniques, page 142), CO 37 sts. Change to size US 7 (4.5 mm) needles. Begin Lace Ribbon Stitch (from text or chart); *work even until you have worked Rows 1-12 of Lace Ribbon Stitch twice.* Change to size US 8 (5 mm) needles; repeat from * to *. Change to size US 9 (5.5 mm) needles; repeat from * to *. Change to size US 10 (6 mm) needles; repeat from * to *. Knit 6 rows. BO all sts using Picot BO.

SECOND SECTION

With RS facing, carefully unravel Provisional CO and place sts on size US 7 (4.5 mm) needle. Begin St st, slipping first st of every row purlwise and working last st in St st.

SHAPE SECTION

NOTE: *Section is shaped using Short Rows (see Special Techniques, page 142).*

SHORT ROWS 1 (RS) AND 2 (WS): Knit to last 4 sts, wrp-t, purl to end.

SHORT ROWS 3 AND 4: Knit to 3 sts before wrapped st, wrp-t, purl to end.

Repeat Short Rows 3 and 4 nine times (11 sts have been wrapped). Knit across entire row, working wraps together with wrapped sts as you come to them. Purl 1 row. Work even in St st until right-hand edge of Section measures 3" (7.5 cm) from beginning of St st, ending with a WS row. Work Short Rows 1 and 2 once, then Short Rows 3 and 4 ten times. Knit across entire row, working wraps together with wrapped sts as you come to them. Purl 1 row.

NEXT ROW (RS): Work as for First Section, beginning after CO.

FINISHING

Block as desired.

LACE RIBBON STITCH

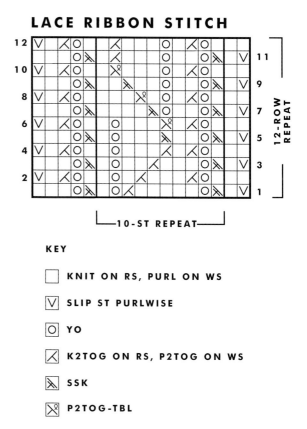

12-ROW REPEAT

10-ST REPEAT

KEY

☐ KNIT ON RS, PURL ON WS

Ⅴ SLIP ST PURLWISE

Ⓞ YO

◪ K2TOG ON RS, P2TOG ON WS

◪ SSK

◪ P2TOG-TBL

GARANCE CAMISOLE

Knitwear is often relegated to the realm of blustery bad weather. Protective outerwear and cozy, insulating layers are certainly where wooly knits excel, but why restrict your handiwork to this domain? When I came across this glowing skein of pure silk, dyed in a flamboyant shade of red-violet, I knew that it had to become something slinky and revealing. A simple trapezoid is knit from the top down in the round with eyelet increases along the sides to encourage floaty drape unfettered by seams. A folded hem neckline holds a simple silk ribbon that can be adjusted to customize fit; it serves as straps and embellishment at once. Channel your inner coquette in this cheeky knit.

SIZES
To fit bust sizes 28 (30, 32, 34, 36)" [71 (76, 81.5, 86.5, 91.5) cm]

FINISHED MEASUREMENTS
26¾ (28¾, 30¾, 32¾, 34¾)" [68 (73, 78, 83, 88.5) cm] below bust

YARN
Neighborhood Fiber Co. Penthouse Silk Fingering [100% silk; 500 yards (457 meters) / 4 ounces (114.5 grams)]: 2 hanks Truxton Circle

NEEDLES
One 24" (60 cm) long or longer circular (circ) needle size US 5 (3.75 mm)

Change needle size if necessary to obtain correct gauge.

NOTIONS
Waste yarn or stitch holder; stitch markers; 6 yards (5.5 meters) silk ribbon, 2½" (6.5 cm) wide

GAUGE
24 sts and 32 rows = 4" (10 cm) in Stockinette stitch (St st)

NOTE
The Back and Front are worked separately from the top down, then they are joined and the Body is worked in the round down to the bottom edge.

STITCH PATTERNS

I-Cord Edging
(panel of 3 sts worked at beginning and end of row; 1-row repeat)
ALL ROWS: At beginning of row, slip 3 sts purlwise wyib; at end of row, p3.

1x1 Rib Flat
(odd number of sts; 1-row repeat)
ROW 1 (RS): K1, *p1, k1; repeat from * to end.
ROW 2: Knit the knit sts and purl the purl sts as they face you.
Repeat Row 2 for *1x1 Rib Flat*.

1x1 Rib in the Round
(even number of sts; 1-rnd repeat)
All Rnds: *K1, p1; repeat from * to end.

Flag Pattern Flat
(multiple of 8 sts + 6; 12-row repeat)
ROW 1 (WS): K3, *p6, k2; repeat from * to last 3 sts, k3.
ROW 2: K3, *p3, k5; repeat from * to last 3 sts, k3.
ROW 3: K3, *p4, k4; repeat from * to last 3 sts, k3.

ROW 4: K3, *p5, k3; repeat from * to last 3 sts, k3.
ROW 5: K3, *p2, k6; repeat from * to last 3 sts, k3..
ROW 6: K3, *p7, k1; repeat from * to last 3 sts, k3.
ROW 7: Repeat Row 5.
ROW 8: Repeat Row 4.
ROW 9: Repeat Row 3.
ROW 10: Repeat Row 2.
ROW 11: Repeat Row 1.
ROW 12: K3, *p1, k7; repeat from * to last 3 sts, k3.
Repeat Rows 1–12 for *Flag Pattern Flat*.

Flag Pattern in the Round

(multiple of 8 sts + 6; 12-rnd repeat)

RND 1: P3, *p2, k6; repeat from * to last 3 sts, p3.

RND 2: K3, *p3, k5; repeat from * to last 3 sts, k3.

RND 3: P3, *p4, k4; repeat from * to last 3 sts, p3.

RND 4: K3, *p5, k3; repeat from * to last 3 sts, k3.

RND 5: P3, *p6, k2; repeat from * to last 3 sts, p3.

RND 6: K3, *p7, k1; repeat from * to last 3 sts, k3.

RND 7: Repeat Rnd 5.

RND 8: Repeat Rnd 4.

RND 9: Repeat Rnd 3.

RND 10: Repeat Rnd 2.

RND 11: Repeat Rnd 1.

RND 12: K3, *p1, k7; repeat from * to last 3 sts, k3.

Repeat Rnds 1–12 for *Flag Pattern in the Round*.

BACK

CO 61 (67, 73, 79, 85) sts.

NEXT ROW (RS): Work I-Cord Edging over 3 sts, work in 1x1 Rib Flat to last 3 sts, work I-Cord Edging to end. Work even in patterns as established until piece measures 4" (10 cm) from the beginning, ending with a RS row.

NEXT ROW (WS): Work I-Cord Edging as established, work in St st, beginning with a purl row, to last 3 sts, work I-Cord Edging to end. Work even for 6 rows.

SHAPE BACK

NEXT ROW (RS): Continuing to work in patterns as established, increase 1 st each side this row, then every 8 rows 8 times, ending with a RS row, and working increased sts in St st as they become available, as follows: Work I-Cord Edging, M1-r, work to last 3 sts, M1-l, work I-Cord Edging to end—79 (85, 91, 97, 103) sts. Transfer sts to stitch holder or waste yarn for Body.

FRONT

Work as for Back until piece measures 4" (10 cm) from the beginning, ending with a RS row and decreasing 1 st on last row—60 (66, 72, 78, 84) sts remain. Place marker 11 (14, 17, 20, 23) sts in from each edge.

NEXT ROW (WS): Work I-Cord Edging as established, work in St st, beginning with a purl row, to first marker, work in Flag Pattern Flat to second marker, work in St st to last 3 sts, work I-Cord Edging to end.

SHAPE FRONT

NEXT ROW (RS): Continuing to work in patterns as established, increase 1 st each side this row, then every 8 rows 8 times, working increased sts in St st as they become available, as follows: Work I-Cord Edging, M1-r, work to last 3 sts, M1-l, work I-Cord Edging to end—78 (84, 90, 96, 102) sts. Do not turn.

BODY

JOIN BACK AND FRONT (RS): With RS facing, transfer Back sts to right-hand end of circ needle. Join for working in the rnd; pm for beginning of rnd. Discontinuing I-Cord Edging, knit across Back sts, pm for side, knit across Front sts to first marker, continue Flag Pattern to next marker, knit to end—157 (169, 181, 193, 205) sts.

SHAPE BODY

NEXT RND: Continuing to work Flag Pattern in the Round (beginning with next rnd after last row of Flag Pattern Flat worked) between center Front markers, and St st on remaining sts, increase 4 sts this rnd, then every 4 rnds 18 times, working increased sts in St st as they become available, as follows: K2, yo, knit to 2 sts before side marker, yo, k2, sm, k2, yo, work to last 2 sts, yo, k2—233 (245, 257,

269, 281) sts. Work even until piece measures 9½" (24 cm) from join, decrease 1 st on last rnd—232 (244, 256, 268, 280) sts remain.

NEXT RND: Change to 1x1 Rib in the Round; work even for 7 rnds. BO all sts in pattern.

FINISHING

Fold CO edge of Back 2" (5 cm) to WS (to beginning of St st), and sew to WS, being careful not to let sts show on RS. Repeat for Front. Thread silk ribbon through Back casing then through Front casing so it starts and ends on the same shoulder.

Block as desired.

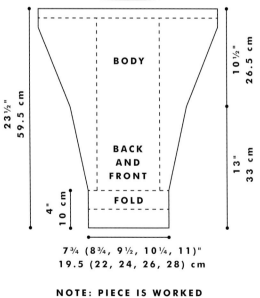

40½ (42½, 44½, 46½, 48½)" HIPS
103 (108, 113, 118, 123) cm

26¾ (28¾, 30¾, 32¾, 34¾)" UNDER BUST
68 (73, 78, 83, 88.5) cm

23½"
59.5 cm

BODY

10½"
26.5 cm

BACK
AND
FRONT

13"
33 cm

FOLD

4"
10 cm

7¾ (8¾, 9½, 10¼, 11)"
19.5 (22, 24, 26, 28) cm

NOTE: PIECE IS WORKED FROM THE TOP DOWN

ISLA CARDIGAN

Many first-time sweater knitters are advised to measure a favorite sweater and use those measurements as a guide. This is wonderful advice and a great entree into design. For the Isla Cardigan I've used this reverse engineering technique to replicate a cotton cardigan I found at a thrift store. I loved all the details—three-quarter-length sleeves, slightly puffed sleevecaps, and an interesting take on an empire waistline.

I wanted to re-create the piece using warmer, more exotic materials (in this case, a possum-merino blend from New Zealand, and vintage buttons). I took some knitterly liberties, eliminating seams by using short-row shaping to create a shoulder slope, and creating a defined pleated ridge at the bustline. I can see knitting many iterations of this simple but fun knit. It is shown at right paired with the Marion Collar (see page 38) and on pages 34 and 35 on its own.

SIZES
To fit bust sizes 31 (33, 35, 37, 39, 41, 45, 49, 53)" [78.5 (84, 89, 94, 99, 104, 114.5, 124.5, 134.5) cm]

FINISHED MEASUREMENTS
33 (35, 37, 39, 41, 43, 47, 51, 55)" [84 (89, 94, 99, 104, 109, 119.5, 129.5, 139.5) cm] bust

YARN
Zealana Rimu DK [60% fine New Zealand merino / 40% possum fibre; 134 yards (123 meters) / 50 grams]: 6 (6, 6, 7, 7, 7, 8, 8, 9) balls #02 Kiwicrush

NEEDLES
One set of five double-pointed needles (dpn) size US 5 (3.75 mm)

One set of five double-pointed needles size US 6 (4 mm)

One 32" (80 cm) long circular (circ) needle size US 5 (3.75 mm)

One pair straight needles size US 6 (4 mm)

Change needle size if necessary to obtain correct gauge.

NOTIONS
Waste yarn or stitch holder; stitch marker; 7 (7, 7, 9, 9, 9, 9, 9, 9) ¾" (19 mm) buttons

GAUGE
20 sts and 24 rows = 4" (10 cm) in Stockinette Stitch (St st), using larger needles

22 sts and 26 rows = 4" (10 cm) in Twisted Rib Flat, using smaller needles, slightly stretched

NOTE
Back of Cardigan is worked with shoulder "tabs" that extend over the shoulders to the front. The Fronts are worked through the armhole shaping, then each Front is gathered, bound off, and sewn to the bound off edge of the Back shoulder "tabs." The Sleeve caps are gathered as well before binding off, creating slightly puffed Sleeves when sewn in.

STITCH PATTERNS

Twisted Rib Flat

(even number of sts; 1-row repeat)

ROW 1 (RS): *K1-tbl, p1; repeat from * to end, end k1-tbl if working over an odd number of sts.

ROW 2: Purl the purl sts tbl and knit the knit sts as they face you.

Repeat Row 2 for *Twisted Rib Flat.*

Twisted Rib in the Round

(even number of sts; 1-rnd repeat)

ALL RNDS: *K1-tbl, p1; repeat from * to end.

BACK

Using smaller circ needles, CO 79 (85, 89, 95, 99, 105, 115, 125, 135) sts. Begin Twisted Rib Flat; work even until piece measures 8 (8, 8½, 8½, 9, 9, 9½, 9½, 10)" [20.5 (20.5, 21.5, 21.5, 23, 23, 24, 24, 25.5) cm] from the beginning, ending with a WS row.

NEXT ROW (RS): Change to larger needles and St st; work even until piece measures 12 (12, 12½, 12½, 13, 13, 13½, 13½, 14)" [30.5 (30.5, 32, 32, 33, 33, 34.5, 34.5, 35.5) cm] from the beginning, increasing 1 (0, 1, 0, 1, 0, 0, 0, 0) st(s) on first row, and ending with a WS row—80 (85, 90, 95, 100, 105, 115, 125, 135) sts.

SHAPE ARMHOLES

NEXT ROW (RS): BO 4 (5, 5, 6, 7, 7, 9, 11, 13) sts at beginning of next 2 rows, 2 sts at beginning of next 0 (0, 0, 0, 0, 0, 2, 4, 6) rows, decrease 1 st each side every other row 2 (2, 4, 5, 5, 6, 6, 6, 4) time(s), then every 4 rows 2 (2, 1, 1, 1, 1, 1, 1, 2) time(s), as follows: K2, k2tog, knit to last 4 sts, ssk, k2—64 (67, 70, 71, 74, 77, 79, 81, 85) sts remain. Work even until armholes measure 6¾ (6¾, 7¼, 7¼, 7¾, 7¾, 8¼, 8¼, 8¾)" [17 (17, 18.5, 18.5, 19.5, 19.5, 21, 21, 22) cm], ending with a WS row.

SHAPE NECK

NEXT ROW (RS): K17 (18, 19, 19, 20, 21, 21, 22, 23) sts, join a second ball of yarn, BO next 30 (31, 32, 33, 34, 35, 37, 37, 39) sts, knit to end. Working both sides at the same time, decrease 1 st at each neck edge on next RS row, then every 4 rows once, as follows: At right neck edge, knit to last 3 sts, k2tog, k1; at left neck edge, k1, ssk, knit to end—15 (16, 17, 17, 18, 19, 19, 20, 21) sts remain each side for shoulders.

SHAPE RIGHT SHOULDER

NOTE: *Shoulders are shaped using Short Rows (see Special Techniques, page 142).*

SHORT ROW 1 (WS): Working on right shoulder sts only (leave left shoulder sts on needle or transfer to st holder if preferred), purl to last 4 (4, 5, 5, 5, 5, 5, 6) sts, wrp-t.

SHORT ROW 2: Knit to end.

SHORT ROW 3: Purl to 4 (4, 4, 4, 4, 5, 5, 5, 5) sts before wrapped st from previous row, wrp-t.

SHORT ROW 4: Knit to end.

SHORT ROWS 5 AND 6: Repeat Short Rows 3 and 4. Place marker at one end of row to mark top of shoulder.

SHAPE FRONT TAB

NEXT ROW (WS): Purl across all sts, working wraps together with wrapped sts as you come to them.

NEXT ROW (RS): Knit to last 2 sts, M1-l, k2—16 (17, 18, 18, 19, 20, 20, 21, 22) sts. Work even until piece measures 4 (4, 4¼, 4¼, 4½, 4½, 4¾, 4¾, 5)" [10 (10, 11, 11, 11.5, 11.5, 12, 12, 12.5) cm] from marker, ending with a WS row. BO all sts.

SHAPE LEFT SHOULDER

SHORT ROW 1 (RS): Knit to last 4 (4, 5, 5, 5, 5, 5, 6) sts, wrp-t.

SHORT ROW 2: Purl to end.

SHORT ROW 3: Knit to 4 (4, 4, 4, 4, 5, 5, 5, 5) sts before wrapped st from previous row, wrp-t.

SHORT ROW 4: Purl to end.

SHORT ROWS 5 AND 6: Repeat Short Rows 3 and 4. Place marker at one end of row to mark top of shoulder.

SHAPE FRONT TAB

NEXT ROW (RS): Knit across all sts, working wraps together with wrapped sts as you come to them. Purl 1 row.

NEXT ROW (RS): K2, M1-r, knit to end—16 (17, 18, 18, 19, 20, 20, 21, 22) sts. Work even until piece measures 4 (4, 4¼, 4¼, 4½, 4½, 4¾, 4¾, 5)" [10 (10, 11, 11, 11.5, 11.5, 12, 12, 12.5) cm] from marker, ending with a WS row. BO all sts.

RIGHT FRONT

Using smaller straight needles, CO 40 (42, 44, 48, 50, 52, 58, 62, 68) sts. Begin Twisted Rib Flat; work even until piece measures 8 (8, 8½, 8½, 9, 9, 9½, 9½, 10)" [20.5 (20.5, 21.5, 21.5, 23, 23, 24, 24, 25.5) cm] from the beginning, ending with a WS row.

NEXT ROW (RS): Change to larger needles and St st; work even until piece measures 12 (12, 12½, 12½, 13, 13, 13½, 13½, 14)" [30.5 (30.5, 32, 32, 33, 33, 34.5, 34.5, 35.5) cm] from the beginning, increasing 0 (1, 1, 0, 0, 0, 0, 0, 0) st(s) on first row, and ending with a RS row—40 (43, 45, 48, 50, 52, 58, 62, 68) sts.

SHAPE ARMHOLE

NEXT ROW (WS): BO 4 (5, 5, 6, 7, 7, 9, 11, 13) sts at armhole edge once, then 2 sts 0 (0, 0, 0, 0, 0, 1, 2, 3) time(s), then decrease 1 st at armhole edge every other row 2 (2, 4, 5, 5, 6, 6, 6, 4) times, then every 4 rows 2 (2, 1, 1, 1, 1, 1, 1, 2) time(s), as follows: Knit to last 4 sts, ssk, k2—32 (34, 35, 36, 37, 38, 40, 40, 43) sts remain. Work even until piece measures 4¾ (4¾, 5, 5, 5¼, 5¼, 5½, 5½, 5¾)" [12 (12, 12.5, 12.5, 13.5, 13.5, 14, 14, 14.5) cm], ending with a WS row.

NEXT ROW (RS): K1 (1, 0, 1, 0, 1, 1, 1, 0), *k2tog; repeat from * to last st, k1—17 (18, 18, 19, 19, 20, 21, 21, 22) sts remain. BO all sts purlwise.

LEFT FRONT

Using smaller straight needles, CO 40 (42, 44, 48, 50, 52, 58, 62, 68) sts. Begin Twisted Rib Flat, beginning with a purl st; work even until piece measures 8 (8, 8½, 8½, 9, 9, 9½, 9½, 10)" [20.5 (20.5, 21.5, 21.5, 23, 23, 24, 24, 25.5) cm] from the beginning, ending with a WS row.

NEXT ROW (RS): Change to larger needles and St st; work even until piece measures 12 (12, 12½, 12½, 13, 13, 13½, 13½, 14)" [30.5 (30.5, 32, 32, 33, 33, 34.5, 34.5, 35.5) cm] from the beginning, increasing 0 (1, 1, 0, 0, 0, 0, 0, 0) st(s) on first row, and ending with a WS row—40 (43, 45, 48, 50, 52, 58, 62, 68) sts.

SHAPE ARMHOLE

NEXT ROW (RS): BO 4 (5, 5, 6, 7, 7, 9, 11, 13) sts at armhole edge once, then 2 sts 0 (0, 0, 0, 0, 0, 1, 2, 3) time(s), then decrease 1 st at armhole edge every other row 2 (2, 4, 5, 5, 6, 6, 6, 4) times, then every 4 rows 2 (2, 1, 1, 1, 1, 1, 1, 2) time(s), as follows: K2, k2tog, knit to end—32 (34, 35, 36, 37, 38, 40, 40, 43) sts remain. Work even until piece measures 4¾ (4¾, 5, 5, 5¼, 5¼, 5½, 5½, 5¾)" [12 (12, 12.5, 12.5, 13.5, 13.5, 14, 14, 14.5) cm], ending with a WS row.

NEXT ROW (RS): K1 (1, 0, 1, 0, 1, 1, 1, 0), *k2tog; repeat from * to last st, k1—17 (18, 18, 19, 19, 20, 21, 21, 22) sts remain. BO all sts purlwise.

SLEEVES

Using smaller dpns, CO 46 (46, 46, 48, 48, 50, 50, 52, 54) sts. Join for working in the rnd, being careful not to twist sts; pm for beginning of rnd. Begin Twisted Rib in the Round; work even until piece measures 2" (5 cm) from the beginning.

NEXT RND: Change to larger dpns and St st, increase 2 sts this rnd, then every 8 (7, 5, 5, 4, 4, 3, 3, 3) rnds 6 (7, 9, 10, 12, 13, 15, 17, 18) times, working increased sts in St st as they become available, as follows: K2, M1-l, knit to last 2 sts, M1-r, k2—60 (62, 66, 70, 74, 78, 82, 88, 92) sts. Work even until piece measures 12" (30.5 cm) from the beginning, ending last rnd 4 (5, 5, 6, 7, 7, 9, 11, 13) sts before marker.

SHAPE CAP

NEXT ROW (RS): BO 8 (10, 10, 12, 14, 14, 18, 22, 26) sts, removing marker, knit to end—52 (52, 56, 58, 60, 64, 64, 66, 66) sts remain. Purl 1 row.

NEXT ROW (RS): Decrease 1 st each side this row, then every 4 rows 6 (6, 7, 8, 8, 9, 9, 10, 10) times, as follows: K2, k2tog, knit to last 4 sts, ssk, k2—38 (38, 40, 40, 42, 44, 44, 44, 44) sts remain. Work even until cap measures 7 (7, 7½, 7½, 8, 8, 8½, 8½, 9)" [18 (18, 19, 19, 20.5, 20.5, 21.5, 21.5, 23) cm], ending with a WS row.

NEXT ROW (RS): K2, ssk, knit to last 4 sts, k2tog, k2—36 (36, 38, 38, 40, 42, 42, 42, 42) sts remain. Purl 1 row.

NEXT ROW (RS): *K2tog; repeat from * to end—18 (18, 19, 19, 20, 21, 21, 21, 21) sts remain. Purl 1 row. BO all sts.

FINISHING

Block as desired. Sew BO edge of Front Tabs to final BO edge of Fronts. Sew in Sleeves. Sew side seams.

NECKBAND

Using smaller circular needle, beginning at lower Right Front edge, pick up and knit approximately 3 sts for every 4 rows, and 1 st for each BO st around neck edge to lower Left Front edge, ending with an odd number of sts. Begin Twisted Rib Flat; work even for 1 row. Place markers for buttonholes on Right Front, the first 1" (2.5 cm) up from lower edge, the last 2" (5 cm) above the end of the ribbing, and the remaining 5 (5, 5, 7, 7, 7, 7, 7, 7) evenly spaced between.

NOTE: *Be sure to place marker before a purl st, so that buttonhole doesn't disrupt flow of ribbing.* BUTTONHOLE ROW (RS): [Work to marker, yo, k2tog] 7 (7, 7, 9, 9, 9, 9, 9, 9) times, work to end. Work even for 3 rows. BO all sts in rib. Sew buttons to Left Front, opposite buttonholes.

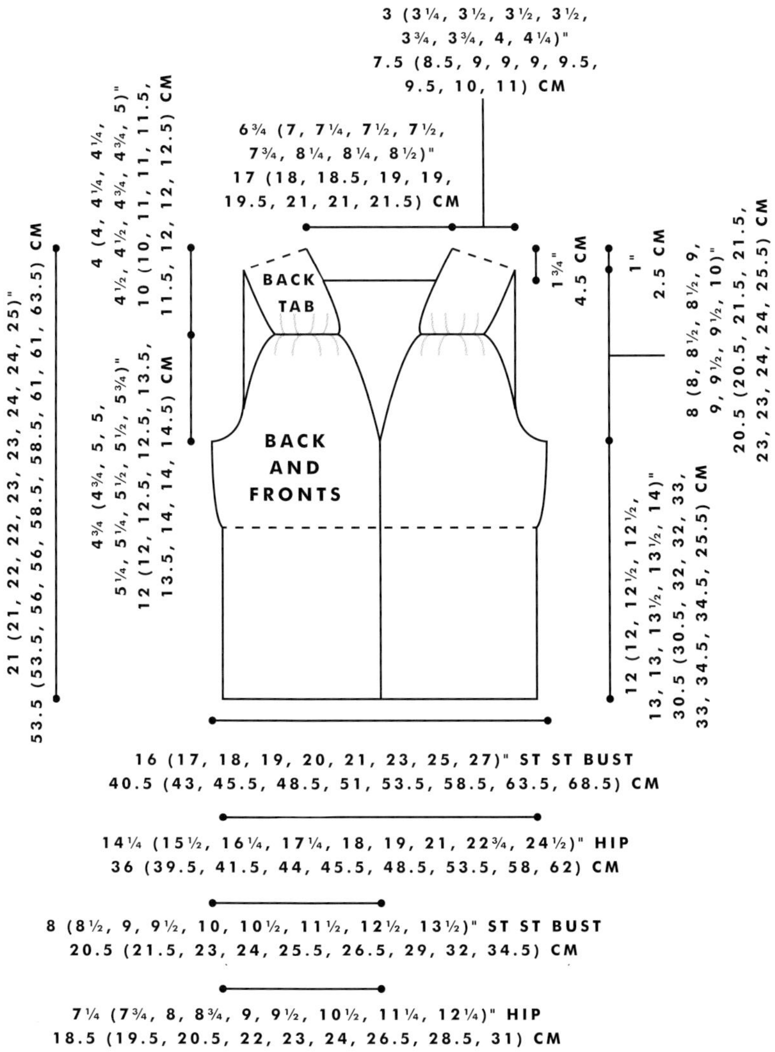
3 (3¼, 3½, 3½, 3½, 3¾, 3¾, 4, 4¼)"
7.5 (8.5, 9, 9, 9, 9.5, 9.5, 10, 11) CM
6¾ (7, 7¼, 7½, 7½, 7¾, 8¼, 8¼, 8½)"
17 (18, 18.5, 19, 19, 19.5, 21, 21, 21.5) CM
21 (21, 22, 22, 23, 23, 24, 24, 25)"
53.5 (53.5, 56, 56, 58.5, 58.5, 61, 61, 63.5) CM
4 (4, 4¼, 4¼, 4½, 4½, 4¾, 4¾, 5)"
10 (10, 11, 11, 11.5, 11.5, 12, 12, 12.5) CM
4¾ (4¾, 5, 5, 5¼, 5¼, 5½, 5½, 5¾)"
12 (12, 12.5, 12.5, 13.5, 13.5, 14, 14, 14.5) CM
BACK TAB
BACK AND FRONTS
1¾"
4.5 CM
1"
2.5 CM
8 (8, 8½, 8½, 9, 9, 9½, 9½, 10)"
20.5 (20.5, 21.5, 21.5, 23, 23, 24, 24, 25.5) CM
12 (12, 12½, 12½, 13, 13, 13½, 13½, 14)"
30.5 (30.5, 32, 32, 33, 33, 34.5, 34.5, 25.5) CM
16 (17, 18, 19, 20, 21, 23, 25, 27)" ST ST BUST
40.5 (43, 45.5, 48.5, 51, 53.5, 58.5, 63.5, 68.5) CM
14¼ (15½, 16¼, 17¼, 18, 19, 21, 22¾, 24½)" HIP
36 (39.5, 41.5, 44, 45.5, 48.5, 53.5, 58, 62) CM
8 (8½, 9, 9½, 10, 10½, 11½, 12½, 13½)" ST ST BUST
20.5 (21.5, 23, 24, 25.5, 26.5, 29, 32, 34.5) CM
7¼ (7¾, 8, 8¾, 9, 9½, 10½, 11¼, 12¼)" HIP
18.5 (19.5, 20.5, 22, 23, 24, 26.5, 28.5, 31) CM

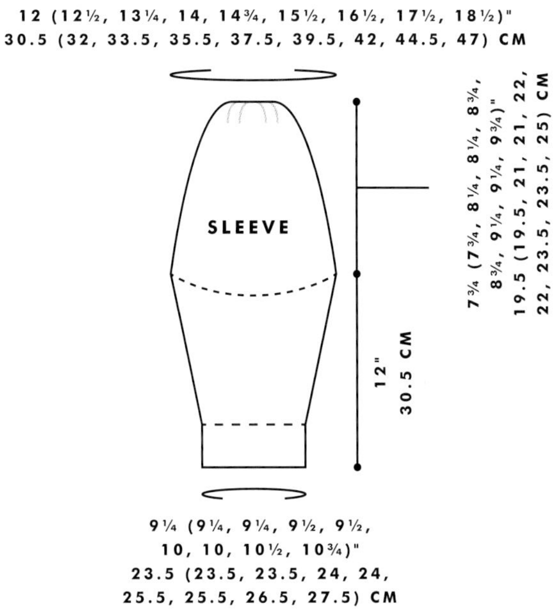
12 (12½, 13¼, 14, 14¾, 15½, 16½, 17½, 18½)"
30.5 (32, 33.5, 35.5, 37.5, 39.5, 42, 44.5, 47) CM
SLEEVE
7¾ (7¾, 8¼, 8¼, 8¾, 8¾, 9¼, 9¼, 9¾)"
19.5 (19.5, 21, 21, 22, 22, 23.5, 23.5, 25) CM
12"
30.5 CM
9¼ (9¼, 9¼, 9½, 9½, 10, 10, 10½, 10¾)"
23.5 (23.5, 23.5, 24, 24, 25.5, 25.5, 26.5, 27.5) CM

MARION COLLAR

This lush chartreuse accessory has an unlikely origin story that starts in Iceland, at the design house Farmers Market. In addition to its signature modern *lopapey-sa*, the boutique had an incredible selection of accessories made from local fur. One item in particular stole my heart, a lush collar with streaks of copper, black, and gold. It looked at home in any ensemble, invoking a feral feeling when paired with worn denim and an upscale vintage vibe when worn with silk.

I know that fur is not for everyone, so I wanted to re-create the shaggy, dramatic piece using wool. Lustrous, colorful, curly locks are the perfect raw material, but knitting them would have dampened their spiraling bounce. Instead, I knit a double-layered base and affixed the locks with a crochet hook, pulling them through one layer. It's a fun, meditative process that I revisited for the Studio Pullover (page 126).

FINISHED MEASUREMENTS

18" (45.5 cm) wide x 3" (7.5 cm) tall

YARN

Schulana Lambswool [100% extrafine lambswool; 109 yards (99.5 m) / 25 grams]: 1 ball #02 (A)

Schulana Angora Fashion Print [80% angora / 20% nylon; 122 yards (111.5 m) / 25 grams]: 1 ball #63 (B)

2 ounces (57 grams) Hippie Chix Fiber Art loose curly locks in color to match B (C)

NEEDLES

One 24" (60 cm) long circular (circ) needle size US 8 (5 mm)

One spare 20" (50 cm) long or longer circular needle size US 8 (5 mm), for Kitchener st

Change needle size if necessary to obtain correct gauge.

NOTIONS

Crochet hook size US H/8 (5 mm); waste yarn; stitch markers; hook and eye closure; tapestry needle (if working Kitchener st)

GAUGE

14 sts and 26 rows = 4" (10 cm) in Stockinette stitch (St st), using 2 strands of A held together

COLLAR

Using crochet hook, waste yarn and Provisional (Crochet Chain) CO (see Special Techniques, page 142), CO 60 sts. Change to 2 strands of A held together. Begin St st, beginning with a purl row.

NEXT ROW (RS): [K20, pm] twice, knit to end. Purl 1 row.

SHAPE COLLAR

INCREASE ROW (RS): Continuing in St st, increase 4 sts this row, then every 4 rows 3 times, as follows: [Knit to 1 st before marker, M1-r, k1, sm, k1, M1-l] twice—76 sts. Work even for 3 rows.

NEXT ROW (WS): Change to 2 strands of B held together and Garter st (knit every row); work even for 3 rows.

DECREASE ROW (RS): Continuing in Garter st, decrease 4 sts this row, then every 4 rows 3 times, as follows: [Knit to 3 sts before marker, ssk, k1, slip marker, k1, k2tog] twice—60 sts remain. Work even for 3 rows.

FINISHING

LOCKS

With RS facing, insert crochet hook into knitted fabric and pull one end of lock through to RS, then move ½" (1.5 cm) in any direction and pull opposite end of lock through to RS. Continue in this manner, pulling locks through randomly until entire RS is covered with locks.

With RS facing, carefully unravel Provisional CO and place sts on empty needle. Using Three-Needle BO or Kitchener st (see Special Techniques, page 141), graft live ends of Collar together. Sew hook and eye closure in place at CO edge, then sew side seams. Block gently if desired.

KARIN FASCINATOR

Fascinators are frivolous, yes, but they're transformative, too. Everyone should own at least a few accessories that completely change their carriage and mood, and for me, a fascinator falls firmly in that category. It's small, it won't keep you warm, and it will probably require some bobby pins and a healthy dose of confidence, but you're guaranteed to feel transported to another era, and to draw smiles and most likely some fun chatter.

FINISHED MEASUREMENTS

Hat: 6½" (16.5 cm) diameter

Veil: 22¼" (56.5 cm) wide x 16" (40.5 cm) tall

YARN

Zealana Performa Kauri Worsted Weight (60% merino / 30% possum / 10% silk; 94 yards (86 meters) / 50 grams): 1 skein each K14 Red Tuhi (A) and K10 Red Waina (B)

Schulana Kid-Paillettes (42% kid mohair / 40% polyester / 18% silk; 137 yards (125.5 meters) / 25 grams): 1 ball #340 Merlot (C)

NEEDLES

One set of five double-pointed needles (dpn) size US 6 (4 mm)

One pair straight needles size US 10 (6 mm)

Change needle size if necessary to obtain correct gauge.

NOTIONS

Stitch marker; sewing needle and thread; bobby pins

GAUGE

20 sts and 22 rows = 4" (10 cm) in Stained Glass Pattern from Chart, using smaller needles

16 sts and 18 rows = 4" (10 cm) in Star Mesh, using larger needles and C

Note: Gauge is not essential for Veil.

STITCH PATTERNS

1x1 Rib

(even number of sts; 1-rnd repeat)

ALL RNDS: *K1, p1; repeat from * to end.

Star Mesh

(multiple of 4 sts + 1; 4-row repeat)

ROWS 1 AND 3 (WS): Purl.

ROW 2: K1, *yo, s2kp2, yo, k1; repeat from * to end.

ROW 4: Ssk, yo, k1, *yo, s2kp2, yo, k1; repeat from * to last 2 sts, yo, k2tog.

Repeat Rows 1–4 for *Star Mesh.*

STAINED GLASS PATTERN

HAT

Using smaller needles and A, CO 70 sts. Join for working in the rnd, being careful not to twist sts; pm for beginning of rnd. Begin 1x1 Rib; work even for 5 rnds.

SHAPE BODY

NEXT RND: *K2, M1; repeat from * to end—105 sts. Knit 1 rnd.

NEXT RND: Change to Stained Glass Pattern from Chart; work even until entire Chart is complete, working decreases as indicated in chart—35 sts remain.

SHAPE CROWN

RND 1: Using A, k2tog, knit to end—34 sts remain.

RND 2: Using B, *k2tog; repeat from * to end—17 sts remain.

RND 3: Using A, k2tog, knit to end—16 sts remain.

RND 4: Using B, *k2tog; repeat from * to end—8 sts remain.

RND 5: Using A, knit.

RND 6: Using B, *k2tog; repeat from * to end—4 sts remain.

RND 7: Using A, k1, k2tog, k1—3 sts remain. Working on these 3 sts, work I-Cord (see Special Techniques, page 141) for 3 rnds.

NEXT RND: K3tog—1 st remains. Fasten off.

FINISHING

Block as desired.

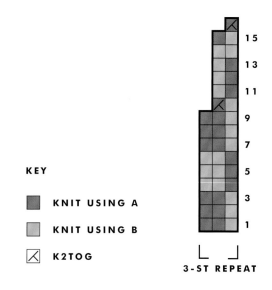

KEY

■ KNIT USING A

■ KNIT USING B

⊠ K2TOG

3-ST REPEAT

VEIL

Using Long-Tail CO (see Special Techniques, page 142), larger needles and C, CO 89 sts, leaving a 12" (30.5 cm) tail. Begin Star Mesh; work even until piece measures 16" (40.5 cm) from the beginning. BO all sts, leaving a 12" (30.5 cm) tail.

FINISHING

Thread CO tail through short side edge and gather edge. Repeat for BO tail and opposite side edge. Block as desired. Using sewing needle and thread, sew one gathered edge of Veil to one side of Hat, then opposite gathered edge to opposite side of Hat. Arrange Veil and tack to Hat in additional spots if needed, making sure it drapes attractively. To wear, use bobby pins to affix Hat with Veil draped to one side.

L'ARBRE HAT + MITTS

I am first and foremost a yarn-driven designer. Since I've spent most of my career promoting specific yarns for the companies that have employed me, I have grown quite used to having very clear parameters. When a yarn like Road to China crosses my path, I tend to reel a bit, but when the "blank slate" jitters subside, I turn to my trusty stitch dictionaries. I fell in love with the simplicity of the textured stitch I chose for the accessories featured here, and I couldn't help but notice its resemblance to trees. Whenever I move to a new place my first priority is finding a forest where I can go for long hikes year-round. I see the same calm, hallowed beauty in a skein of luxury fibers, expertly spun and dyed, so this pairing is an homage to that parallelism.

FINISHED MEASUREMENTS

Mitts: 7" (18 cm) circumference

Hat: 19½" (49.5 cm) circumference

YARN

The Fibre Company Road to China worsted [65% baby alpaca / 15% silk / 10% camel/ 10% cashmere; 69 yards (63 meters) / 50 grams]: 4 hanks Lapis

Note: You will need 2 hanks each for Hat and Mitts.

NEEDLES

Mitts and Hat: One set of five double-pointed needles (dpn) size US 8 (5 mm)

Hat: One 16" (40 cm) circular (circ) needle size US 8 (5 mm)

Change needle size if necessary to obtain correct gauge.

NOTIONS

Stitch markers; small stitch holder (Mitts)

GAUGE

18 sts and 24 rows = 4" (10 cm) in Little Tree Pattern

ABBREVIATION

WLS (WORK LOOSE STRAND): Insert right-hand needle under loose strand from Rnd 2 (strand will lay across right-hand needle) and knit the next st, drawing tip of right-hand needle back under loose strand so that it sits behind st just knit.

STITCH PATTERNS

1x1 Rib

(even number of sts; 1-rnd repeat)

ALL RNDS: *K1, p1; repeat from * to end.

Little Tree Pattern

(multiple of 8 sts; 4-rnd repeat)

RNDS 1 AND 3: *K5, p3; repeat from * to end.

RND 2: Slip 5 wyif, k3 (being careful not to pull strand in front of slipped sts too tightly); repeat from * to end.

RND 4: *K2, WLS, k5; repeat from * to end.

Repeat Rnds 1–4 for *Little Tree Pattern*.

MITTS

WRIST

Using dpns, CO 32 sts. Join for working in the rnd, being careful not to twist sts; pm for beginning of rnd. Begin 1x1 Rib; work even for 6 rnds.

NEXT RND: Change to Little Tree Pattern; work even until piece measures approximately 6½" (16.5 cm) from the beginning, ending with Rnd 4.

HAND

SHAPE THUMB GUSSET

RND 1: K1, M1-r, k3, M1-l, k1, p3, pm, work in Little Tree Pattern as established to end—34 sts.

RND 2: Knit to marker, work to end.

RND 3: K1, M1-r, k5, M1-l, k1, p3, work to end—36 sts.

RND 4: Repeat Rnd 2.

RND 5: K1, M1-r, k7, M1-l, k1, p3, work to end—38 sts.

RND 6: K11 and transfer to st holder, CO 5 sts using Backward Loop CO (see Special Techniques, page 141), p3, work to end—32 sts.

NEXT RND: Working Little Tree Pattern across all sts, work even until piece measures 1" (2.5 cm) from Thumb opening, ending with Rnd 1 or 4 of Little Tree Pattern.

NEXT RND: Change to 1x1 Rib; work even for 6 rnds. BO all sts in pattern.

FINISHING

Block as desired.

HAT

Using circ needle, CO 88 sts. Join for working in the rnd, being careful not to twist sts; pm for beginning of rnd. Begin 1x1 Rib; work even until piece measures 1" (2.5 cm) from the beginning.

NEXT RND: Change to Little Tree Pattern; work even until piece measures 6½" (16.5 cm) from the beginning, ending with Rnd 2.

SHAPE CROWN

NOTE: *Change to dpns when necessary for number of sts on needle.*

RND 1: *K1, s2kp2, k4; repeat from * to end—66 sts remain.

RND 2: *K1, WLS, k4; repeat from * to end.

RND 3: *K3, p3; repeat from * to end.

RND 4: *Slip 3 wyif, k3; repeat from * to end.

RND 5: Repeat Rnd 3.

RND 6: *K1, WLS, k4; repeat from * to end.

RND 7: *K3, p3tog; repeat from * to end—44 sts remain.

RND 8: *Slip 3 wyif, k1; repeat from * to end.

RND 9: *K3, p1; repeat from * to end.

RND 10: *K1, WLS, k2; repeat from * to end.

RND 11: *K3, p1; repeat from * to end.

RND 12: *S2kp2, k1; repeat from * to end—22 sts remain.

RND 13: *K1, p1; repeat from * to end.

RND 14: *K2tog; repeat from * to end—11 sts remain.

Cut yarn, leaving a 12" (30.5 cm) tail. Thread tail through sts twice, pull tight, and fasten off.

FINISHING

Block as desired.

COLOR ME BRAVE

WHAT DOES IT MEAN TO HAVE GOOD COLOR SENSE? COLOR IS
SO INTENSELY EMOTIONAL, AND IT IS OFTEN TIED TO OUR SENSE
OF STYLE. THE CONFIDENCE YOU HAVE IN YOUR OWN SENSE OF
STYLE DIRECTLY CORRELATES TO HOW COMFORTABLE YOU ARE
PLAYING WITH COLOR, BUT THE FASHION MACHINE IS SET UP TO
MAKE SURE YOU'RE NEVER COMFORTABLE—COLOR TRENDS SHIFT
CONSTANTLY TO CREATE A SENSE OF NEWNESS. THE CONSUMER
IS TASKED WITH EITHER KEEPING UP OR DROPPING OUT. OR
TAKE THE THIRD, UNSPOKEN OPTION, WHICH IS TO CONNECT
WITH YOUR PERSONAL PREFERENCES AND BOLDLY WEAR THOSE,
IGNORING THE OPPRESSIVE RHYTHMS OF TRENDS. DIY-ERS HAVE
A DISTINCT ADVANTAGE WHEN NAVIGATING THE SERPENTINE
AND SEEMINGLY ARBITRARY RECOMMENDATIONS OF FASHION
ADVISORS, BUT THERE IS STILL PLENTY OF APPREHENSION WHEN
FACED WITH A JAM-PACKED LYS, BRIMMING WITH RAW MATERIALS
IN AN OVERWHELMING AND COMPREHENSIVE SPECTRUM. I CAN'T
TELL YOU HOW MANY TIMES I WAS ASKED DURING MY TENURE AT
THE YARN EMPORIUM WEBS IN NORTHAMPTON, MASSACHUSETTS,
"WHICH COLOR SHOULD I CHOOSE?!"

More often than not, the panicked knitter was holding up a skein in a color she was
already wearing. This taught me that people knit what they know. It happens with our
regular clothing purchases, too. We know that we need that jersey T-shirt in "our" blue.
Certain colors become our signatures, and there is nothing wrong with this. The trouble
crops up when we take a personal inventory and find that we're essentially knitting
carbon copies and never daring to try a color that might enliven our entire look.

So how do you develop the bravery needed to look current, but more importantly,
fabulous? I think it is an ongoing process, and a delightful one at that. The first step is
to take an honest look at your color predilections. You might already be aware of your
biases, but if you have never thought about it, check out your closet or your Ravelry
pages (provided they have up-to-date images from your stash and WIP pile). Do you
see a sea of gray or a riotous mix of prints? What's missing from the equation?

When I am choosing colors for a new line of yarn, I always think about Roy G. Biv, the acronym taught in grade school science and art classes to help children remember the color spectrum: red, orange, yellow, green, blue, indigo, violet. I rarely interpret this literally, but it serves as an organizing principle to make sure I'm not leaving out something vital. There is often a temptation to skip bringing in colors that don't sell as well—traditionally brown, yellow, and orange—but I fight for these colors! Palettes that leave them out can tend to look unbalanced or, worse, unexciting.

It's possible that you do have a strong sense of what looks good on you, or what you favor. You might even hate certain colors and avoid them. It's worth examining these choices and for that I recommend the classic manual that divides people into "seasons," *Color Me Beautiful*. Still in print and largely unchanged after 30 years, it offers a sound theory of how color can affect your appearance. The basis for the theory comes from artist Johannes Itten's observation that most people are instinctively drawn toward the colors that flatter them. We know which shades make us look sickly and which ones draw compliments, but Itten's research illuminates the science behind this occurrence.

The most compelling bit of advice in the book might be the palettes. It's notable that each palette contains almost all of the colors in the Roy G. Biv spectrum. But the clear banana yellow that can be worn by a high-contrast Winter is very different from the golden ochre advised for a warm-toned Autumn. I'll never forget the moment I realized red lipstick didn't have to look garish on me—it clicked when I found the right version of red for my complexion, a rusty orange red. (A visit to a makeup counter isn't a bad place to start experimenting with what works for you.)

When I'm asked what my favorite color is, I always refuse to answer. This is because there is almost always a version of a color that I like and wear. Before dismissing an entire color, consider all the variations and iterations that exist. This flexibility is especially useful when dealing with seasonal trends. Using trendy colors is often risky for the hand-knitter, since the trend cycle might outpace the knitting process. It makes sense to select yarns for larger projects in colors that will remain in your personal stable for more than a season or two. Reserve the flashy, more controversial shades for smaller accessories.

When it comes to combining colors, keep your eyes open, but don't be afraid to use technology. When I see a textile that I love, I use the myPantone app to isolate the shades that are used. It's a fantastic way to come up with color combinations for stripes or colorwork. Some combinations are so effective and well-loved that they acquire nicknames like "grellow," a portmanteau of gray and yellow. This particular combination utilizes the principle of pairing an acidic bright with a subdued neutral, or "juicies and blahs," to borrow the parlance of the ladies behind Mason-Dixon Knitting. Joelle Hoverson of Purl Soho has also managed to establish a modern classic combination of creamy whites and beiges and vibrating neons. It all hinges on proportion here—the teaspoon of lime juice that perks up a plate of steamed fish.

Speaking of food, don't overlook the inspirational power of the grocery store or the farmers' market. From labels to produce displays, the bounty of nature can be an incredible jumping-off point for color inspiration. Take your camera and snap a photo of anything that calls out to you. Don't overthink it, just photograph. Most likely, a pattern will emerge and you'll uncover unlikely favorites. When color is isolated from garments and skeins of yarns you can respond to it in a purer way, without the intimidating possibility of making an expensive wardrobe mistake. You'll find that your shopping becomes more edited as you bypass colors that you find appealing but aren't doing you any favors. If something languishes in your stash or your wardrobe, it is often because it falls outside of your most flattering range.

Once you have established your core palette, you can refresh your wardrobe easily with just a few pieces. These could be inspired by trends, or you could find yourself inspired by something more specific or personal. I often find myself in color phases that are set off by a stranger's outfit or a house's paint job. Noticing a vibrant shade or novel combination will quickly snowball and you'll start to "see" it everywhere. Buy nail polish or tights in these new-to-you shades. Those are low-investment ways to make your staple items seem completely modern. Knitting a smaller piece—a chunky hat, fingerless gloves, even a short, boxy sweater—in an *au courant* color can instantly elevate the gray dress you've worn for six seasons. Bind-off a button band using an extreme color, knowing that you can always go back later and replace it with a more classic hue. Most of all, keep at it. Color sense is a dynamic, multi-pronged skill that should never stay static.

THINK LIKE A STYLIST

STYLING IS A JOB THAT MOST PEOPLE HAVE NEVER HEARD OF AND EVEN FEWER PEOPLE UNDERSTAND. I CERTAINLY DIDN'T KNOW WHAT IT WAS UNTIL I WAS REQUIRED TO JUMP IN AND TRY MY HAND AT STYLING A PHOTO SHOOT. WHAT SEEMED LIKE AN OVERWHELMING, AMORPHOUS TASK QUICKLY BECAME ONE OF MY FAVORITE DUTIES. STYLING IS A BLANKET TERM FOR A PASSEL OF TASKS THAT ARE ALL IN SUPPORT OF THE "SHOT," THE ELUSIVE PHOTO OF A GARMENT, MODEL, OR ITEM THAT WILL EMOTIONALLY MOVE THE VIEWER. THE STYLIST IS RESPONSIBLE FOR GATHERING, ORGANIZING, AND UTILIZING ALL MANNER OF PERIPHERAL OBJECTS, FROM UNDERPINNINGS TO BACKDROPS TO PROPS. HOWEVER, THE MOST IMPORTANT TOOLS IN A STYLIST'S BELT AREN'T TANGIBLE AT ALL—THEY ARE IMAGINATION AND AN "EYE."

While I was working with Norah Gaughan at Berroco Inc. I cultivated a styling technique that involved assigning a "story" to a specific pattern collection. I would search for images that illustrated my narrative and create a mood board. I would often have one or two "holy grail" images that held all of the DNA for the look I was after. If a photo shoot is an attempt at storytelling, the mood board is the script, and it ensures there will be no misunderstanding when communicating a concept to the photographer, makeup artist, and model. Outfit ideas, location or pose possibilities, hair and makeup—no detail is too insignificant for the mood board.

With this in place, I would gather the croquis (garment sketches), small reelings of the yarns used (for color matching), and, lastly, a shopping list. Starting with undergarments and moving outward, I'd list what we absolutely needed, what I thought would work well and, lastly, a few wish list items. And then I'd shop. And shop. Until I literally dropped. The shopping happened online, in thrift stores, at the mall, in boutiques, in my own closet and any other willing friends' closets. The more I prepared, the more room there was for magic on the day of the shoot, but shopping can never cover all bases. Impromptu acquirement, like a wildflower bouquet picked on location, can upstage all the accessories in my arsenal.

The photo shoot for this book was one of the first where I was not solely in charge of styling. It was an incredible gift to have someone else managing this formidable task, and even better, it was wonderful to have a skilled, sophisticated voice entirely different from my own. While I selected Emilie Maslow based on an impressively gorgeous

portfolio, I had no idea how she would perceive my knits or the inspiration images on my mood boards, which included bonfires, sulky models, street-style snaps, and watercolor illustrations of ravens.

I was ecstatic with what Emilie brought to the table. Not only did she completely understand the touch points I'd shared with her, she pushed me outside of my comfort zone. I was slated to model, and when she dressed me, I felt elevated. Her vision gave me verve and energy. A good stylist can tap into your sartorial fantasies and help you realize them, even ones you didn't know you had, like my "luxe lumberjack" look seen with the Levitt Hat (page 110). Emilie understood the humor inherent in the juxtaposition of rustic marled handspun cashmere knit into a simple skull-hugging hat. A silky plaid shirt and a simple but gorgeous fur vest completed the backwoods gone upscale story. Similarly, Erin Skipley, the hair and makeup stylist, knew exactly what I meant when I said our Magpie knitter should look like a girl who had wandered off into the woods at an outdoor wedding. As we pulled polishes with the shimmery complexity of a beta fish, she managed to transform our model (see above) into a ramshackle-glam Biba girl, achieving the exact look I was after.

I've learned a lot from styling photo shoots and working with accomplished stylists and makeup artists like Emilie and Erin, and these lessons have crept into my daily life. Here are some pointers that I hope will help you.

FOR ORGANIZATION
(AND TO MAKE SURE YOU CAN SEE AND ACCESS WHAT YOU HAVE)

- Organize your closet by garment type, from skimpiest to heaviest (camisoles to long-sleeved collared shirts, mini-skirts to full dresses) and then by color.

- Store scarves and belts on hangers made for the purpose. When things are in plain sight, you're more likely to wear them.

- Sweaters should never be hung because this can stretch them out of shape. I store them rolled on a shelf so I can easily see the color and texture.

- Know when to let an item go and get rid of it. I'm not particularly good at this because I can always imagine a future use for even the strangest items. I wait for the occasional ruthless mood to strike.

- Store seasonal and special-occasion items by themselves but don't put them out of bounds entirely. Tights and sweaters can extend the life of summer dresses and shorts, and a sparkly evening gown can be dressed down with a T-shirt or sweater.

FOR WHEN YOU HIT THE ROAD

- Begin a list with the number of days you'll be away. If you know what you'll be doing, add that to the list, as well as a weather projection. Tally up the number of outfits you'll need to build. It never hurts to overpack undergarments and basic tops.

- I treat packing like planning for a shoot or dressing a character. Keeping a cohesive look amongst pieces makes mixing and matching easier. It's also a fun way to edit your wardrobe and try on a new persona while you're literally out of your comfort zone.

- My secret weapon travel pieces are usually a bit of a security blanket. An oversized cardigan, a generous cowl, or a wide wool square shawl can serve as blanket, pillow, coat, and accessory. Choose a neutral color and it will serve you through a whole trip.

- Take time to visit local boutiques and, of course, yarn stores. Clothing and yarn can be the best souvenirs—visual reminders of your journey, even more so if you find something unique to the locale.

FOR YOUR NEXT SHOPPING SPREE

- Treat your next shopping trip as a trendspotting expedition. Note which silhouettes are crossing barriers and appearing in multiple places. Use these cues to pick your next knitting pattern, or to determine what will set you apart from a sea of ponchos or berets. Visit Karen Templer's Fringe Association blog for fantastic coverage of trends in knitwear. Karen spots the currents and digs through Ravelry for matches.

- Veer from your usual path. Seek out unique, one-off boutiques, if only for inspiration. Observe how things are presented but don't take it as gospel.

- Try shopping alone. It might not feel like as much fun as shopping with a friend, but you'll have the quiet focus needed to channel your inner muse.

- When you return home with your spoils, take the opportunity to do a little closet maintenance. Find one item to donate for each item you're adding, or refresh the organization. Don't overly favor any new items; instead, mix them in with existing pieces to reinvigorate.

FOR WHEN YOU NEED AN UPDATE

- If your usual fare is feeling stale, consider adding a piece that is over-the-top ridiculous. My Karin Fascinator (page 40) fits the bill. This tiny decorative hat doesn't exactly serve a purpose, and it's a completely outmoded piece of haberdashery. People wil stop you in the street to talk about it, and you might feel a bit conspicuous at first, but hold your head high. In the gray climes of Seattle, I consider it my civic duty to wear bright colors and whimsical accessories.

- Window shopping is easier than ever thanks to sites like Pinterest. I create "Dream Wardrobe" boards for each season and try not to overthink it. Rather than getting a staid, proscribed list from a magazine or mannequin, I scroll through and pin impulsively, operating on a gut level. I may end up purchasing a piece or two, but more than anything the boards function as repositories for ideas.

- It's all too easy to get stuck in a rut, cranking out reliable iterations of a beloved pattern or silhouette. Remember to step back on occasion and reestablish what works for your body type and current style. Remember the easy alterations in every knitter's purview—length is a simple edit that can make a huge difference. If you love wearing cuff bracelets or a riot of rings, shorten sleeves to show them off. If you tend toward empire-waist dresses, eliminate inches from a sweater for a cute cropped length.

- Don't be afraid to reconfigure old knits. Try them on upside down, backward, or inside out. You'd be surprised how often it works, especially when a sweater has lots of ease or an unusual construction. Pick up stitches and knit new length in an entirely different color and texture, or add fabric or fiber patches with the hooking technique shown in the Studio Pullover (page 126) and Marion Collar (page 38).

FOR WHEN YOU WANT TO DRESS UP YOUR KNITS

- Stylists are generally layering experts, and knitters share this skill. Wearing hardy, classic wool often requires a base layer to guard against itchy fibers. Why not perk up your pullovers with long-sleeved underpinnings in a bold, on-trend color or a classic black-and-white stripe? Try a flowy silk tunic under fitted cardigans or plaid blouses under cable-heavy accessories. Adding textures and pattern to your already dazzling knits only ups the ante.

- Scour thrift stores for vintage pins. Adding a bit of oversized sparkle will up the glam factor. My favorite way to wear a scarf is looped once with one corner of one tail fastened to its counterpart with a pin, then pulled to the side so the pin rests on one shoulder— elegant and secure with a slight hint of ramshackle chic.

- Surface crochet is my favorite way to mimic embroidery on knits. Using a crochet hook with the yarn held at the wrong side, chain stitch onto your fabric, working from the right side. Make freeform squiggles or create a foundation for additional embellishment. I've used torn T-shirt fabric, silk ribbon, and beads to add improvised floral appliqués to otherwise down-to-earth knitwear.

FOR TIME SPENT CLOSE TO HOME

Homebodies

MY FRIEND AND FELLOW FIBER ADDICT JARED HAS A THEORY—ALL KNITTERS ARE INTROVERTS.

I tend to agree with him. Introversion doesn't necessarily mean antisocial, as any fiber event will reveal. Knitters are happy to congregate and revel with the best of them, but we excel at nesting, too. What makes us such happy homebodies?

The comforts of home and the comforts of knitting are nearly interchangeable. Knitting is a steadfast companion that happens to be portable—a bit of home that you can stuff into a sack and take with you. Sitting in a bustling airport or waiting room isn't nearly as noisome when you unpack the contents of your knitting bag. Knitting will transport you back to the place where most of us are at our happiest—on a couch, surrounded by humble accoutrements: tea, a movie, and a pet add up to otherworldly happiness.

Knitting tends to seep into the decor of the truly obsessed. Needles, notions, and stash yarn are hard to contain, so it must be displayed in an artful, inspiring way. I have my formidable book collection organized by color. Beauty trumps utility in this (book)case. Investing in a dress form might feel like an indulgence, but besides being an invaluable tool, it blends seamlessly into my decor. When I'm not using it to work out proportions and fit, I dress it with my latest knit. The beautiful linen-covered form has a cast-iron base and it announces that a maker lives here. I've also decided that some tools should be within reach at all times—double-pointed needles in every size, for instance. Displayed in a vintage jar in a variety of materials and sizes, they resemble a utilitarian bouquet. One of my favorite decorations is tall cones of yarn direct from the mill. These stately, outsized pillars are reminders that yarn is beautiful even when unknit.

Items knit for the home—blankets, pillows, kitchen accessories—are a natural extension of the knitter's queue, and a blessed respite from the trials of fit and finishing. When you feel like communing with yarn but you don't want to bother with the hassles of a full-sized garment, knitting a simple item like the Borgarnes Pillow will serve as a calming break between larger projects and a chic addition to your favorite knitting chair.

As for garments to wear at home, I believe in something just a notch above a well-loved sweatshirt, like the loose Meta Tee. The silhouettes and the knitting should be carefree, and the fabrics should be comfortable and easy. Wool-cotton blends and plump single-ply merino are ideal candidates—cushiony and temperate with lots of tactile appeal. The Loro Vest is a prime example of the sort of garment I like to wear on a lazy weekend. It's essentially a wearable blanket, thick with texture and draft-blocking features. It's entirely comfortable, but I wouldn't feel underdressed leaving the house to get provisions…for a cozy evening in, of course.

LORO VEST

It can be a fool's game to try to predict what will be a hit with knitters. So-called wildfire knits can take on a life of their own. This was certainly the case with my Aidez cardigan, a free pattern that has been knit thousands of times. When I try to dissect the appeal, I land on a few key points. The basic construction is blessedly simple, and the neck-hugging shawl collar is universally flattering. Secondly, it was an easy knit. Macro cables were speedy and dramatic when knit with a round, outsized yarn.

It felt wonderful to revisit these elements here with a buoyant hand-dyed merino. I've simplified the back, which is now a clean swath of moss stitch, putting all focus on the deeply tactile plaited cables on each front. These dramatic braids are flanked by a simple column of easy lace.

SIZE
Small (Medium, Large)

FINISHED MEASUREMENTS
31 (37, 41)" [78.5 (94, 104) cm]

YARN
Madelinetosh Tosh Merino [100% superwash merino wool; 210 yards (192 meters) / 3½ ounces (100 grams)]: 6 (7, 8) hanks Calligraphy

NEEDLES
One pair straight needles size US 9 (5.5 mm)

One spare needle size US 9 (5.5 mm) for Three-Needle BO

Change needle size if necessary to obtain correct gauge.

NOTIONS
Cable needle; stitch markers

GAUGE
16 sts and 26 rows = 4" (10 cm) in Moss Stitch

ABBREVIATIONS
C10B: Slip 5 sts to cable needle, hold to back, k5, k5 from cable needle.

C10F: Slip 5 sts to cable needle, hold to front, k5, k5 from cable needle.

STITCH PATTERNS

Moss Stitch
(even number of sts; 4-row repeat)
ROWS 1 (RS) AND 2: *K1, p1; repeat from * to end.
ROWS 3 AND 4: *P1, k1; repeat from * to end.
Repeat Rows 1–4 for *Moss Stitch.*

Right Ribbing Panel
(panel of 9 sts; 2-row repeat)
ROW 1 (RS): K2, p2, k2, p3.
ROW 2: K3, p2, k2, p2.
Repeat Rows 1 and 2 for *Right Ribbing Panel.*

Left Ribbing Panel
(panel of 9 sts; 2-row repeat)
ROW 1 (RS): K3, p2, k2, p2.
ROW 2: K2, p2, k2, p3.
Repeat Rows 1 and 2 for *Left Ribbing Panel.*

Faggoting
(panel of 2 sts; 1-row repeat)
ALL ROWS: Yo, p2tog.

Plaited Cable
(panel of 15 sts; 14-row repeat)
ROWS 1, 5, 7, 9, AND 11 (RS): Knit.
ROW 2 AND ALL WS ROWS: Purl.
ROW 3: C10B, k5.
ROW 13: K5, C10F.
ROW 14: Purl.
Repeat Rows 1–14 for *Plaited Cable.*

BACK

CO 74 (86, 94) sts.

ROW 1 (RS): Slip 1 knitwise tbl, k1 (edge sts), work in Moss st to last 2 sts, k2 (edge sts).

ROW 2: Slip 1 knitwise tbl, k1, work to last 2 sts, k2.

Work even in Moss st, working edge sts at beginning and end of every row as established, until piece measures 2" (5 cm) from the beginning, ending with a WS row.

SHAPE BACK

NEXT ROW (RS): Continuing in patterns as established, decrease 2 sts this row, then every 12 rows 11 times, as follows: Work 2 sts, ssk, work to last 4 sts, k2tog, work to end—50 (62, 70) sts. Work even as established until piece measures 24 (25, 26)" [61 (63.5, 66) cm] from the beginning, ending with a WS row. BO all sts in pattern.

FRONTS (BOTH ALIKE)

CO 53 (59, 63) sts. Knit 4 rows.

ROW 1 (RS): Slip 1 knitwise tbl, k1 (edge sts), work Right Ribbing Panel over 9 sts, Faggoting over 2 sts, p6 (9, 11), pm, work Plaited Cable over 15 sts, pm, p6 (9, 11), work Faggoting over 2 sts, Left Ribbing Panel over 9 sts, k2 (edge sts). Work even in patterns as established, working edge sts as for Back, and sts on either side of Plaited Cable in Rev St st, until piece measures 6" (15 cm) from the beginning, ending with a RS row.

SHAPE FRONT

NEXT ROW (WS): Continuing in patterns as established, decrease 2 sts this row, every 6" (15 cm) twice, then every 3" (7.5 cm) once, as follows: Work to 2 sts before marker, ssk, work to next marker, k2tog, work to end—45 (51, 55) sts remain. Work even until piece measures 30 (32½, 34½)" [76 (82.5, 87.5) cm] from the beginning, ending with a WS row. Transfer sts to spare needle for first Front; leave sts on needle for second Front. Set aside.

FINISHING

With RS of Fronts facing, pm 15 (15½, 16)" [38 (39.5, 40.5) cm] up from CO edge for side seam and 6 (7½, 8)" [15 (19, 20.5) cm] down from BO edge for neck seam, along right side edge on Right Front and left side edge on Left Front. Place markers 15 (15½, 16)" [38 (39.5, 40.5) cm] up from CO edge along both sides of Back. Sew side seams from CO edge to side seam markers. With WSs together (RSs facing out), using Three-Needle BO (see Special Techniques, page 142), join live sts of both Fronts (seam will be on RS). Sew side edge of Fronts to BO Back neck edge, between neck seam markers.

Block as desired.

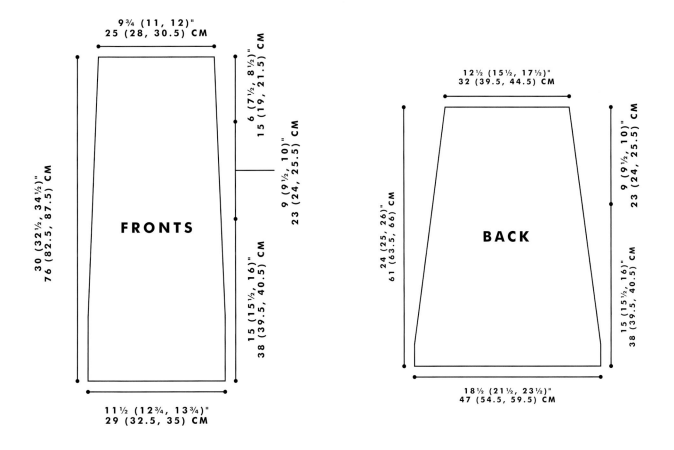

TASSE MUG/PINT COZY

This little cozy was borne out of frugality and sentimentality. Besides yarn and nail polish, the only thing I really collect is mugs. I am also very clumsy, which means I have broken the handles off at least a half dozen of my favorites. Rather than toss these damaged vessels, I now use a ceramic file to smooth sharp edges and a simple ribbed cozy to insulate my hand against the hot liquid inside. I was happily surprised one day when I realized that the same cozies could also protect my fingers from the cold of a frozen pint of ice cream. Noro Kureyon is one of my all-time favorite yarns, and knitting from opposite ends of a center-pull cake allows me to explore the masterful color shifts in an entertaining lifted rib.

FINISHED MEASUREMENTS
10½" (26.5 cm) circumference x 3" (7.5 cm) tall

YARN
Noro Kureyon [100% wool; 108 yards (99 meters) / 1¾ ounces (50 grams)]: 1 ball #328

NEEDLES
One set of five double-pointed needles (dpn) size US 7 (4.5 mm)

One set of five double-pointed needles size US 6 (4 mm)

Change needle size if necessary to obtain correct gauge.

NOTIONS
Stitch marker

GAUGE
20 sts and 25 rows = 4" (10 cm) in Lifted Two-Color Rib, using smaller needles

NOTE
Divide yarn into two equal balls; one ball will be yarn A, the other will be yarn B.

STITCH PATTERNS
Lifted Two-Color Rib
(even number of sts; 2-rnd repeat)
RND 1: Using A, *k1, p1, repeat from * to end.
RND 2: Using B, *k1 into row below, p1; repeat from * to end.
Repeat Rnds 1 and 2 for *Lifted Two-Color Rib*.

BODY

Using smaller needles and A, CO 40 sts. Divide sts evenly among 4 needles. Join for working in the rnd, being careful not to twist sts; pm for beginning of rnd. Knit 1 rnd. Begin Lifted Two-Color Rib; work even until piece measures 1½" (4 cm) from the beginning. Change to larger needles; work even until piece measures 2¾" (7 cm) from the beginning, ending with Rnd 1 of Lifted Two-Color Rib. Purl 1 rnd. BO all sts purlwise.

BOTTOM (OPTIONAL)

With WS of Body facing, using smaller needles and B, pick up and knit 40 sts along CO edge (this will create a ridge on the RS). Join for working in the rnd; pm for beginning of rnd.

SHAPE BOTTOM

RND 1 AND ALL ODD-NUMBERED RNDS: Knit.

RND 2: *K6, k2tog; repeat from * to end—35 sts remain.

RND 4: *K5, k2tog; repeat from * to end—30 sts remain.

RND 6: *K4, k2tog; repeat from * to end—25 sts remain.

RND 8: *K3, k2tog; repeat from * to end—20 sts remain.

RND 10: *K2, k2tog; repeat from * to end—15 sts remain.

RND 12: *K1, k2tog; repeat from * to end—10 sts remain.

Cut yarn, leaving a 12" (30.5 cm) tail. Thread tail through sts twice, pull tight, and fasten off.

FINISHING

Block as desired.

KOSI COWL

Sadly, "the shoemaker's daughter has no shoes" is an adage I relate to all too well. Most of my knit samples are photographed and then sent around the country in trunk shows. They rarely come back to me, so when I have the chance to purchase a piece of hand-knitting, I jump, especially when it serves double duty as an accessory and inspiration.

My Kosi Cowl was inspired by a cowl I purchased in Iceland, designed and knit by an unknown knitter as part of a fund-raising effort. I swapped warm, fuzzy Icelandic wool for Balance Bulky, a chunky organic wool and cotton blend from O-Wool. The original was knit in a wintry palette of off-white, neutral brown, cerulean, and ash gray-blue. It struck me as utterly modern and idiosyncratic, the same combination I strove for with my color choices.

FINISHED MEASUREMENTS
84" (213.5 cm) long x 8" (20.5 cm) wide

YARN
O-Wool Balance Bulky [50% certified organic merino wool / 50% certified organic cotton; 106 yards (97 meters) / 3½ ounces (100 grams)]: 1 hank each #1000 Natural (A), #2109 Turquoise (B), #8001 Smoky Quartz (C), #4001 Cinnabar (D)

NEEDLES
One pair straight needles size US 10 (6 mm)

Change needle size if necessary to obtain correct gauge.

NOTIONS
Crochet hook size US J/10 (6 mm); waste yarn; tapestry needle (if working Kitchener st)

GAUGE
14 sts and 20 rows = 4" (10 cm) in Garter stitch (knit every row)

STITCH PATTERN
Rib and Garter Pattern
(multiple of 4 sts; 20-row repeat)
ROW 1 (RS): Slip 1 purlwise, *k2, p2; repeat from * to last 3 sts, k3.
ROW 2: Slip 1 purlwise, *p2, k2; repeat from * to last 3 sts, p3.

ROWS 3–10: Repeat Rows 1 and 2.
ROWS 11–20: Knit.
Repeat Rows 1–20 for *Rib and Garter Pattern*.

COWL

Using crochet hook, waste yarn, and Provisional (Crochet Chain) CO (see Special Techniques, page 142), CO 28 sts. Change to A. Purl 1 row. Begin Rib and Garter Pattern; work even until piece measures approximately 21" (53.5 cm) from the beginning, ending with Row 12, 14, 16, or 18 of Rib and Garter Pattern.

NEXT ROW (RS): Change to B; work even until piece measures 37" (94 cm) from the beginning, ending with Row 12, 14, 16, or 18 of pattern.

NEXT ROW (RS): Change to A; work even until piece measures approximately 45" (114.5 cm) from the beginning, ending with Row 12, 14, 16, or 18 of pattern.

NEXT ROW (RS): Change to C; work even until piece measures approximately 62" (157.5 cm) from the beginning, ending with Row 12, 14, 16, or 18 of pattern.

NEXT ROW (RS): Change to D; work even until piece measures approximately 84" (213.5 cm) from the beginning, ending with Row 20 of pattern.

NEXT ROW (RS): Change to A; knit 1 row.

FINISHING

With RS facing, carefully unravel Provisional CO and place sts on empty needle. Using Three-Needle BO or Kitchener st (see Special Techniques, page 141) and A, join live ends of Cowl together.

Block as desired.

LANA COWL

Cowls have topped the trendy accessory list for many seasons now, and it's easy to see the appeal. The cozy loop of fabric that never needs adjusting is an easy fix for a boring outfit and an effortless way to broadcast your love for yarn. They're just as welcome at home when lounging around a drafty house, denying that the time for radiators and hot water bottles is nigh. The Lana Cowl is proportioned to offer just a little warmth and a flattering bit of color. The stitch pattern has a distinctive right and wrong side, both attractive. Cat Bordhi's Moebius cast-on creates a permanent built-in half-twist, so that both sides are on display. This method takes a bit of patience to get going, but once underway, the knitting is enchanting.

FINISHED MEASUREMENTS

Approximately 32" (81.5 cm) circumference x 8½" (21.5 cm) tall

YARN

The Fibre Company Organik [70% organic merino / 15% baby alpaca / 15% silk; 98 yards (89.5 meters) / 1¾ ounces (50 grams)]: 3 hanks Coral Reef

NEEDLES

One 40" (100 cm) long circular (circ) needle size US 8 (5 mm)

One 40" (100 cm) long circular needle size US 10 (6 mm)

Change needle size if necessary to obtain correct gauge.

NOTIONS

Stitch marker; cable needle (optional)

GAUGE

17 sts and 26 rows = 4" (10 cm) in Little Twist Honeycomb, using smaller needle

ABBREVIATIONS

RT: Slip 1 st to cable needle and hold to back, k1, k1 from cable needle. To work without a cable needle, knit into second st, leaving st on needle, then knit into first st, slipping both sts from needle together.

LT: Slip 1 st to cable needle and hold to front, k1, k1 from cable needle. To work without a cable needle, insert right-hand needle from back to front between first 2 sts, and knit into second st, leaving st on needle, then knit into first st, slipping both sts from needle together.

STITCH PATTERNS

Little Twist Honeycomb

(multiple of 4 sts; 8-rnd repeat)

RND 1: *P1, k2, p1; repeat from * to end.

RND 2: *RT, LT; repeat from * to end.

RNDS 3–5: *K1, p2, k1; repeat from * to end.

RND 6: *LT, RT; repeat from * to end.

RNDS 7 AND 8: Repeat Rnd 1. Repeat Rnds 1–8 for *Little Twist Honeycomb*.

1x1 Rib

(even number of sts; 1-rnd repeat)

ALL RNDS: *K1, p1; repeat from * to end.

COWL

Using smaller needle and Cat Bordhi's Moebius CO (see Special Techniques, page 141), CO 300 sts and knit 1 rnd (2 rings), making sure to end rnd when marker is on left-hand needle tip, not on cable.

NEXT RND: Change to Little Twist Honeycomb; work even until piece measures approximately 7½" (19 cm) from the beginning, ending with Rnd 8 of pattern.

NEXT RND: *K2tog, p2tog; repeat from * to end—150 sts remain.

NEXT RND: Change to 1x1 Rib; work even for 4 rnds. BO all sts in pattern.

FINISHING

Block as desired.

TISANE TANK

One of the most valuable design lessons I ever learned from my friend Norah Gaughan was that it isn't always necessary to reinvent the wheel. Instead, develop a design vocabulary, and if something works, explore the idea, shifting slightly to create new but recognizable versions. The Tisane Tank is a fraternal twin to the Garance Camisole (page 28) and a good example of how yarn choice can change the feel of a garment completely. Fibre Company's Savannah, an unusual blend of wool, cotton, linen, and soya, is worked in a garter ribbing that recalls comforting winter thermals.

SIZES

X-Small (Small, Medium, Large, 1X-Large)

FINISHED MEASUREMENTS

33¼ (37¼, 41¼, 45¼, 49¼)" [84.5 (94.5, 105, 115, 125) cm] bust

YARN

The Fibre Company Savannah DK [50% wool / 20% cotton / 15% linen / 15% soya; 160 yards (146.5 meters) / 50 grams]: 4 (5, 6, 7, 9) hanks Persimmon

NEEDLES

One 24" (60 cm) long circular (circ) needle size US 6 (4 mm)

One 24" (60 cm) long circular needle size US 7 (4.5 mm)

One 24" (60 cm) long circular needle size US 8 (5 mm)

Change needle size if necessary to obtain correct gauge.

NOTIONS

Locking ring stitch markers; waste yarn or stitch holder; 60" (152.5 cm) ribbon, 2½" (6.5 cm) wide

GAUGE

22 sts and 28 rows = 4" (10 cm) in Stockinette stitch (St st), using size US 6 (4 mm) needle

20 sts and 32 rows = 4" (10 cm) in Seeded Rib, using size US 6 (4 mm) needle

NOTES

The Bodice is worked in the round in one piece to the armholes, then Back and Front are worked back and forth to the casing. The Body is picked up from the bodice and worked in the round down to the bottom edge, with Body shaping worked by using increasingly larger needles.

STITCH PATTERNS

Seeded Rib in the Round

(multiple of 2 sts; 2-rnd repeat)

RND 1: Knit.

RND 2: [K1, *k1, p1; rep from * to 2 sts before marker, k2] twice.

Repeat Rnds 1 and 2 for *Seeded Rib in the Rnd.*

Seeded Rib Flat

(multiple of 2 sts + 3; 2-row repeat)

ROW 1 (WS): P1, *p1, k1: repeat from * to last 2 sts, p2.

ROW 2: Knit.

Repeat Rows 1 and 2 for *Seeded Rib Flat.*

1x1 Rib

(even number of sts; 1-rnd repeat)

ALL RNDS: *K1, p1; repeat from * to end.

BODICE

Using size US 6 (4 mm) needle, CO 83 (93, 103, 113, 123) sts, pm for side, CO 83 (93, 103, 113, 123) sts—166 (186, 206, 226, 246) sts. Join for working in the rnd, being careful not to twist sts; pm for beginning of rnd. Begin Seeded Rib in the Round; work even until piece measures 3" (7.5 cm) from the beginning, ending with Rnd 2 of pattern.

DIVIDE FOR FRONT AND BACK

NEXT ROW (RS): K83 (93, 103, 113, 123) and place on waste yarn or st holder for Front, knit to end—83 (93, 103, 113, 123) sts remain for Back.

BACK

Working back and forth in Seeded Rib Flat on Back sts only, work even for 1 row.

SHAPE ARMHOLES

NEXT ROW (RS): Decrease 1 st each side this row, then every 6 rows twice, as follows: Ssk, work to last 2 sts, k2tog—77 (87, 97, 107, 117) sts remain. Work even until armholes measure 7 (7, 7½, 7½, 8)" [18 (18, 19, 19, 20.5) cm], ending with a WS row, decreasing 1 st on last row—76 (86, 96, 106, 116) sts remain.

NEXT ROW (RS): Change to St st; work even until armholes measure 9 (9, 9½, 9½, 10)" [23 (23, 24, 24, 25.5) cm], ending with a WS row. Bind off all sts.

FRONT

Rejoin yarn to sts on hold for Front. Work as for Back until armholes measure 3 (3, 2½, 2½, 2½)" [7.5 (7.5, 6.5, 6.5, 6.5) cm], ending with a WS row.

SHAPE NECK

NEXT ROW (RS): K39 (44, 49, 54, 59), join a second ball of yarn, M1-l, knit to end—39 (44, 49, 54, 59) sts remain for each Front. Working both sides at the same time, work even until armholes measure 7 (7, 7½, 7½, 8)" [18 (18, 19, 19, 20.5) cm], ending with a WS row, decrease 1 st at each armhole edge on last row—38 (43, 48, 53, 58) sts remain for each Front.

NEXT ROW (RS): Change to St st; complete as for Back.

BODY

With RS of Bodice facing, using size US 6 (4 mm) circ needle, and beginning even with right armhole (beginning of rnd for Bodice), pick up and knit 1 st for every CO st of Bodice—166 (186, 206, 226, 246) sts. Join for working in the rnd; pm for beginning of rnd and after 83 (93, 103, 113, 123) sts.

INCREASE RND: K31 (36, 40, 45, 49), [k1-f/b] 20 (20, 22, 22, 24) times, knit to end—186 (206, 228, 248, 270) sts [103 (113, 125, 135, 147) sts for Front, 83 (93, 103, 113, 123) sts for Back].

NEXT RND: Continuing in St st (knit every rnd), work even for 3" (7.5 cm).

NEXT RND: Change to size US 7 (4.5 mm) circ needle; work even for 3" (7.5 cm).

NEXT RND: Change to size US 8 (5 mm) circ needle; work even for 2½ (3, 3, 3½, 3½)" [6.5 (7.5, 7.5, 9, 9) cm].

NEXT RND: Change to 1x1 Rib; work even for ½" (1.5 cm). BO all sts in pattern.

FINISHING

Fold BO edge of Back 1" (2.5 cm) to WS (to beginning of St st), and sew to WS, being careful not to let sts show on RS. Repeat for Fronts. Thread silk ribbon through Right Front, Back, then Left Front casings, so that ends meet at center Front.

Block as desired.

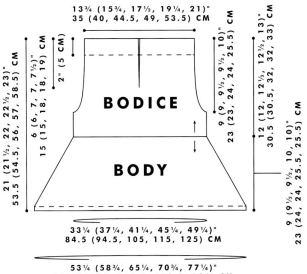

13¾ (15¾, 17½, 19¼, 21)"
35 (40, 44.5, 49, 53.5) CM

2" (5 CM)

9 (9, 9½, 9½, 10)"
23 (23, 24, 24, 25.5) CM

12 (12, 12½, 12½, 13)"
30.5 (30.5, 32, 32, 33) CM

6 (6, 7, 7, 7½)"
15 (15, 18, 18, 19) CM

21 (21½, 22, 22½, 23)"
53.5 (54.5, 56, 57, 58.5) CM

BODICE

BODY

9 (9½, 9½, 10, 10)"
23 (24, 24, 25.5, 25.5) CM

33¼ (37¼, 41¼, 45¼, 49¼)"
84.5 (94.5, 105, 115, 125) CM

53¼ (58¾, 65¼, 70¾, 77¼)"
135.5 (149, 165.5, 179.5, 196) CM

META TEE

Yarns made from T-shirt jersey seem to have a limited but potent appeal. The obvious choices seem to be home décor and simply knotted accessories. Sweaters have always been deemed improbable, most likely because of the heft of the finished fabric. I love the impact of macro-sized stitches and took on the challenge of designing a sweater that wouldn't sag under its own weight. Knitting from side to side on large needles gave me the open, airy look I wanted with minimal droop. A firmly crocheted side seam adds stability and a decorative edge, while trim sleeves, knit at a tighter gauge than the body, neaten the overall appearance.

SIZES
To fit bust sizes 32–34 (36–38, 40–42, 44–46, 48–50)" [81.5–86.5 (91.5–96.5, 101.5–106.5, 112–117, 122–127) cm]

FINISHED MEASUREMENTS
40 (44, 48, 52, 56)" [101.5 (112, 122, 132, 142) cm] bust

Note: Finished fabric is very stretchy.

YARN
HiKoo Tee-Cakes [51% cotton scraps / 49% scraps of undetermined fiber content; 75 yards (68.5 meters) / 225–300 grams]: 4 (4, 4, 5, 5) balls Multi (MC); 1 ball Greys (A)

NEEDLES
One set of five double-pointed needles (dpn) size US 15 (10 mm)

One 24" (60 cm) circular (circ) needle size US 17 (12.75 mm)

Change needle size if necessary to obtain correct gauge.

NOTIONS
Crochet hook size US N/P/15 (10 mm); waste yarn; locking ring stitch markers; sewing needle and thread

GAUGE
8 sts and 10½ rows = 4" (10 cm) in Stockinette stitch (St st), using smaller needles

6 sts and 6¾ rows = 4" (10 cm) in Stockinette stitch, using larger needles

NOTES
Tee is worked sideways in one piece, with an opening for the neck. Sleeves are picked up and worked in the round from the top down, then side seams are worked together using a crochet hook.

If it is necessary to join a new strand of yarn in the middle of a row, overlap old and new strands and sew together using sewing needle and thread.

Because Tee is worked from side to side, it is essential to match row gauge.

BODY

RIGHT FRONT/BACK

Using larger needles and MC, CO 64 (66, 70, 70, 72) sts. Begin St st, slipping first st of every row purlwise and working last st of every row in St st (selvage sts); work even until piece measures 5 (6, 6½, 7½, 8)" [12.5 (15, 16.5, 19, 20.5) cm] from the beginning, ending with a RS row.

SHAPE NECK OPENING

NEXT ROW (WS): Work 32 (33, 35, 35, 36) sts, join a second ball of yarn, work to end.

NEXT ROW: Working both sides at the same time, and working selvage sts at beginning and end of each section, work even until neck opening measures 10 (10, 11, 11, 12)" [25.5 (25.5, 28, 28, 30.5) cm], ending with a WS row. Cut first ball of yarn.

LEFT FRONT/BACK

NEXT ROW (RS): Work across all sts with 1 ball of yarn; continuing in St st, working selvage sts as established, work even until piece measures 5 (6, 6½, 7½, 8)" [12.5 (15, 16.5, 19, 20.5) cm] from end of neck opening, ending with a WS row. BO all sts.

SLEEVES

Lay piece flat without stretching; place markers along CO and BO edges at shoulder. Place additional markers 5 (6, 7, 8, 9)" [12.5 (15, 18, 20.5, 23) cm] to either side of shoulder markers; remove shoulder markers. With RS facing, using dpns and A, pick up and knit 20 (24, 28, 32, 36) sts between markers. Join for working in the rnd; pm for beginning of rnd. Begin St st (knit every rnd); work even for 5 (3, 3, 2, 1) rnd(s).

SHAPE SLEEVE

NEXT RND: Decrease 2 sts this rnd, then every 5 (4, 2, 2, 2) rnds 2 (3, 4, 5, 6) times, as follows: K1, k2tog, knit to last 3 sts, ssk, k1—14 (16, 18, 20, 22) sts remain. Work even until piece measures 6½ (6½, 5½, 5½, 5½)" [16.5 (16.5, 14, 14, 14) cm]. Purl 1 rnd. BO all sts purlwise.

FINISHING

Block as desired. Using markers, join bottom Front and Back corners.

Using crochet hook and A, join sides as follows: Fold Body at shoulders so that WSs are together (RSs facing) and neck opening is at left edge. Make a slip knot and place it on crochet hook. Hold working yarn behind both layers of fabric. From front of work, *insert hook through both layers of fabric, take hook under working yarn from front to back, and draw yarn on hook back through fabric and previous st on hook to form new st. Repeat from *, joining layers of fabric with evenly spaced decorative slip stitches, until you reach the Sleeve.

If desired, after weaving in ends, sew ends in place using sewing needle and thread (optional).

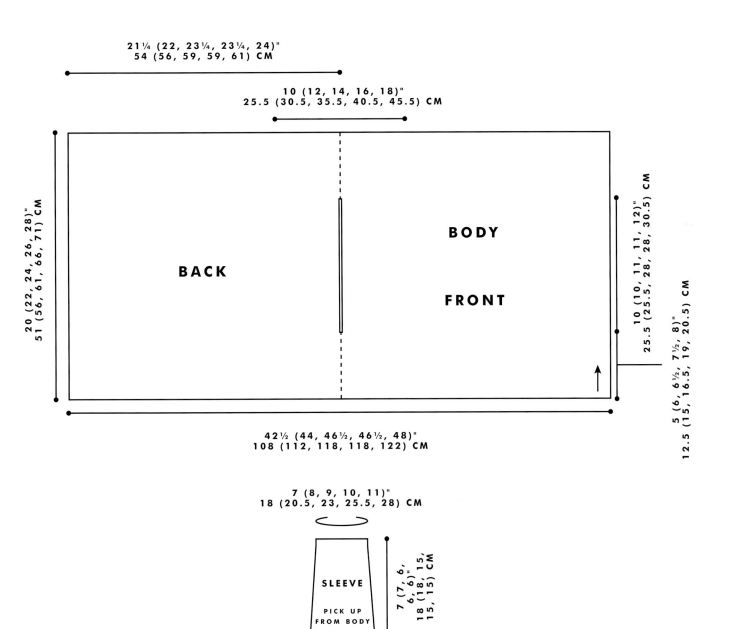

21¼ (22, 23¼, 23¼, 24)"
54 (56, 59, 59, 61) CM

10 (12, 14, 16, 18)"
25.5 (30.5, 35.5, 40.5, 45.5) CM

BODY

BACK

FRONT

20 (22, 24, 26, 28)"
51 (56, 61, 66, 71) CM

10 (10, 11, 11, 12)"
25.5 (25.5, 28, 28, 30.5) CM

5 (6, 6½, 7½, 8)"
12.5 (15, 16.5, 19, 20.5) CM

42½ (44, 46½, 46½, 48)"
108 (112, 118, 118, 122) CM

7 (8, 9, 10, 11)"
18 (20.5, 23, 25.5, 28) CM

SLEEVE

PICK UP
FROM BODY

7 (7, 6, 6, 6)"
18 (18, 15, 15, 15) CM

10 (12, 14, 16, 18)"
25.5 (30.5, 35.5, 40.5, 45.5) CM

HEIMA SLIPPERS

These elfin house shoes are a simplified riff on traditional Icelandic garter-stitch insoles. These detailed wool inserts were at one time given as gifts to travelers wearing soft shoes made of sheep or fish leather. Journeys were measured in how many pairs of insoles and shoes had been worn through.

My hybridization shoe starts with an unembellished but shapely insole. Stitches are picked up and knit in the round with precise shaping and decorative sections of garter stitch. Humble but handsome, they're finished with a simple silk ribbon, but they could just as easily be embellished with embroidery, beadwork, or intarsia, as with the Icelandic originals.

SIZES
Small (Medium, Large)

FINISHED MEASUREMENTS
7 (8, 9)" [18 (20.5, 23) cm] foot circumference
9 (9¾, 10¾)" [86.5 (96.5, 106.5) cm] foot length

YARN
Schoppel-Wolle Relikt [70% wool / 30% nylon; 137 yards (125 meters) / 50 grams]: 2 (2, 3) balls #5875 Olive

NEEDLES
One 16" (40 cm) long circular (circ) needle size US 5 (3.75 mm)

One set of five double-pointed needles (dpn) size US 5 (3.75 mm)

Change needle size if necessary to obtain correct gauge.

NOTIONS
Stitch markers in two colors; 1 yard (1 meter) 2"-wide silk ribbon (optional)

GAUGE
20 sts and 36 rows = 4" (10 cm) in Garter stitch (knit every row)

20 sts and 32 rows = 4" (10 cm) in Stockinette stitch (St st)

NOTE
The Sole is worked in Garter st first, then sts are picked up around the outside edge of the Sole for the Foot. The Toe Box is worked back and forth, then the piece is joined in the round, with shaping for Instep.

SOLE

CO 10 (13, 15) sts. Knit 8 rows.

SHAPE HEEL END

INCREASE ROW: K1, M1-r, knit to last st, M1-l, k1—12 (15, 17) sts. Knit 8 rows.

DECREASE ROW: K1, ssk, knit to last 3 sts, k2tog, k1—10 (13, 15) sts remain. Continuing in Garter st (knit every row), work even until you have 41 (45, 49) rows from the beginning.

SHAPE TOE END

INCREASE ROW: Increase 1 st each side this row, then every 4 rows twice, as follows: K1, M1-r, knit to last st, M1-l, k1—16, (19, 21) sts. Work even until you have 76 (84, 92) rows from the beginning.

DECREASE ROW: Decrease 1 st each side this row, then every 3 rows once, as follows: K1, ssk, knit to last 3 sts, k2tog, k1—12 (15, 17) sts remain. You should have 80 (88, 96) rows from the beginning. BO all sts; do not cut yarn.

FOOT

Using circ needle and yarn attached to Sole, pick up and knit 1 st in each Garter st ridge along long side edge of Sole, working toward heel, pm, pick up and knit 10 (13, 15) sts from CO sts, pm, pick up and knit 1 st in each Garter st ridge along remaining side edge, pm, pick up and knit 12 (15, 17) sts from BO sts—102 (116, 128) sts. Join for working in the rnd; pm of a different color for beginning of rnd.

SHAPE FOOT

NEXT RND: Knit to first marker, work in Garter st (purl 1 rnd, knit 1 rnd) to second marker, knit to third marker, work in Garter st to end.

DECREASE RND: Continuing to work pattern as established, decrease 4 sts this rnd, then every other rnd 4 times, as follows: K1, k2tog, knit to 3 sts before first marker, ssk, k1, sm, work in Garter st as established to next marker, sm, k1, k2tog, knit to 3 sts before next marker, ssk, k1, sm, knit to end—82 (96, 108) sts remain. Slip last 12 (15, 17) sts worked to dpn, removing markers on either side of sts on dpn (only heel markers remain).

SHAPE TOE BOX

Change to working back and forth.

DECREASE ROW 1 (WS): P11 (14, 16), p2tog (1 st from dpn together with 1 st from circ needle), turn—81 (95, 107) sts remain.

DECREASE ROW 2 (RS): Knit to last st on dpn, ssk (1 st from dpn together with 1 st from circ needle), turn—80 (94, 106) sts remain.

Repeat Decrease Rows 1 and 2 thirteen (17, 19) times; do not turn on final repeat of Decrease Row 2—54 (60, 68) sts remain.

SHAPE INSTEP

NEXT RND (RS): Change to working in the rnd; knit to first heel marker, continue in Garter st as established to second heel marker, knit to dpn, pm, knit sts from dpn onto circ needle; pm for beginning of rnd.

DECREASE RND: Decrease 2 sts this rnd, every 3 (2, 2) rnds 3 (6, 5) times, then every 2 (0, 1) rnd(s) 2 (0, 2) times, as follows: K1, ssk, knit to first marker, work in Garter st to second marker, knit to 3 sts before third marker, k2tog, k1, sm, knit to end—42 (46, 52) sts remain.

LEG

NEXT RND: Change to Garter st across all sts; work even for 6 rnds. BO all sts.

FINISHING

Block as desired.

Cut ribbon in half. Weave one piece of ribbon randomly through each slipper, approximately 1½" (4 cm) below top edge (optional; see photo). Tie in bow or knot; trim ends if necessary.

BORGARNES PILLOW

My first few years in the yarn industry coincided with the tail end of the novelty yarn craze of the 2000s. The pendulum swung back toward classic yarns for nearly a decade, but restless knitters have started to crave unusual materials again. The new novelties are much more likely to contain a good dose of natural fiber, and in the case of yarns made from T-shirt jersey, an element of upcycling eco-awareness.

Tactile appeal is also a common denominator; knitters are no longer interested in knitting difficult, itchy metallics or fussy, gimmicky fibers. Yarn made from jersey knits feels as comfortable as your favorite old T-shirt, which makes it an ideal candidate for a throw pillow. Using two shades and an easy-to-work slip-stitch pattern, this pillow makes a unique housewarming gift. This is a case where the stitch pattern changes considerably on the "wrong" side, so choose flat horizontal stripes or nubbly vertical stripes before sewing on buttons.

FINISHED MEASUREMENTS
15" (38 cm) square

YARN
HiKoo Tee-Cakes [51% cotton scraps / 49% scraps of undetermined fiber content; 75 yards (68.5 meters) / 225-300 grams]: 1 ball each Greys (A) and Whites (B)

NEEDLES
One 24" (60 cm) long circular (circ) needle size US 13 (9 mm)

One spare needle size US 13 (9 mm), for Three-Needle BO

Change needle size if necessary to obtain correct gauge.

NOTIONS
Stitch marker; 15" (38 cm) square pillow form; three 1½" (4 cm) buttons

GAUGE
8½ sts and 18 rows = 4" (10 cm) in Bicolor Stripe

NOTES
The RS of the Bicolor Stripe is a smooth fabric with a thin horizontal stripe, while the WS is a nubbly vertical stripe. You can choose which you prefer before finishing the Pillow. Be sure to weave in all ends on whichever side you choose for your WS.

STITCH PATTERN
Bicolor Stripe
(even number of sts; 2-rnd repeat)
RND 1: Using B, *k1, slip 1 purlwise wyif; repeat from * to end.

RND 2: Using A, *slip 1 purlwise wyif, k1; repeat from * to end.
Repeat Rnds 1 and 2 for *Bicolor Stripe*.

PILLOW

Using A, CO 64 sts. Join for working in the rnd, being careful not to twist sts; pm for beginning of rnd. Knit 1 rnd. Begin Bicolor Stripe; work even until piece measures 1" (2.5 cm) from the beginning.

BUTTONHOLE RND: Work 3 sts, [BO next 2 sts, work 9 sts] twice, BO next 2 sts, work to end.

NEXT RND: Work even, casting on 2 sts over BO sts on first rnd using Backward Loop CO (see Special Techniques, page 141), until piece measures 15" (38 cm) from the beginning, ending with Rnd 1 of Bicolor Stripe. Cut yarn.

FINISHING

Decide which side (inside or outside) of work will be the RS. Turn work so that your preferred RSs are together. Divide live sts in half and slide each half to separate ends of circ needle. Using Three-Needle BO (see Special Techniques, page 142) and A, join halves. Block as desired. Sew buttons opposite buttonholes. Insert pillow form.

SURROUND YOURSELF

A FRIEND ONCE SHARED A BIT OF ADVICE HE'D GLEANED FROM HIS FATHER: SURROUND YOURSELF WITH TALENTED PEOPLE. THE LOGIC WAS THAT BESIDES BEING AMAZED AND ENTERTAINED, YOU'D LEARN AND HOPEFULLY BE INSPIRED TO EXPLORE YOUR OWN PASSIONS. I THINK THE SAME GOES FOR STYLE, AND I'VE NEVER LIMITED THIS TO PEOPLE I HAVE IMMEDIATE ACCESS TO, OR EVEN PEOPLE WHO DEAL EXCLUSIVELY IN FASHION OR KNITTING. IN FACT, I FIND MY MOST PROMISING SPARKS OF IMAGINATION FAR OUTSIDE OF THE TEXTILE WORLD. MAKING CONNECTIONS BETWEEN DISPARATE ART FORMS IS ACTUALLY A WONDERFUL WAY TO REINVIGORATE ONE'S OWN WORK OR AESTHETIC. DEVELOPING DESIGN SENSE IS A CONSTANT. HERE ARE JUST A FEW OF MY TALENTED, ALBEIT IMAGINARY, FRIENDS...

Filmmaker **MICHEL GONDRY** has a passionate reverence for the handmade. He often forgoes special effects, choosing to make things from humble materials like toilet paper rolls. In *La Science des Revês*, or *The Science of Sleep*, the main character falls in love with a crafter and rhapsodizes: "I love her because she makes things. You know? She makes things with her hands. It's as if her synapses was married directly to her fingers. Like this. In this way." If that isn't reason enough to watch his films, watch for the adorable sweaters worn by Charlotte Gainsbourg—Aran mini-dresses, marled pullovers, and more.

Icelandic singer **BJÖRK** is a fiercely individualistic beauty who has never felt the need to conform to traditional beauty standards. She also feels no need to continue along a path—she seems to change tack with every album, improving all the time. Her connection with the natural world lends a raw primitivism to her music that I find very useful when designing. She uses clothing as a tool—an extension of whatever she is expressing in a given moment—and while her daring, imaginative outfits are far from practical, I often find elements I can distill into something more approachable.

Illustrator, photographer, and blogger **GARANCE DORÉ** is the epitome of cool. She manages to be impossibly chic and self-deprecating, which makes her simultaneously admirable and relatable. She took a circuitous path to her current career, which is a pastiche of disparate talents that all add up to a very appealing whole. She writes about fashion and beauty with laidback enthusiasm in a way that makes it feel accessible for women of all income and fashion literacy levels.

New York Times fashion photographer **BILL CUNNINGHAM** essentially invented street-style photography and is a tireless observer of trends. He is a sartorial egalitarian, refusing to classify dos and don'ts. Rather, he delights in the variation he sees on city streets and celebrates it. Borrow a page from his book and never leave home without a notebook or a way to photograph the inspiration that surrounds you.

British makeup artist **LISA ELDRIDGE** reminds me of the importance of research and the value of knowing one's history. Her illuminating YouTube tutorials are full of references to famous fashion editorials; I almost always have to look up a fashion photographer or model after watching them. She shows that you can mine the past for ideas with surprisingly fresh results.

FRIDA KAHLO inspired my obsession with folk costume. I use her outfits as a portal to my own Mexican heritage. Her dramatic outfits were anachronistic at the time but they pleased her and were an integral part of her identity as an artist. Kahlo viewed herself as a canvas and a palette, painting her casts and adorning her hair with crowns of flowers. Whenever I feel a bit overdressed, I think of her and add red lipstick.

The work of filmmaker **SOFIA COPPOLA** is unabashedly feminine. Soft and ethereal, the films are nevertheless grounded in solid, affecting emotion. I love *Marie Antoinette* for its opulent excess and *Lost in Translation* for reminding me how powerful it can be to walk without aim.

The late **ALEXANDER MCQUEEN** was a master of the macabre, tapping into the intense beauty of the grotesque and alien all around us. Studying his pieces provokes astonishment and awe. More than pieces of clothing, they are works of art. Pushing the boundaries of scale and proportion are just two of the lessons to be learned; I look forward to gleaning much more from repeated viewing.

I feel a kinship with the idiosyncratic Mulleavy sisters of **RODARTE**, perhaps because they happen to be Mexican, Italian, and Irish like me, or perhaps because they've always shown a special fondness for intricate mixed-media knitwear. They're obsessed, as I am, with obscure cinema, and they tend to favor artistry and history over trends. It lends their work a gravitas that belies their years.

LISA SOLBERG is an L.A.-based artist who bravely works on a large scale with strong color. Her process and the finished work has a certain physicality involved, as she finds herself climbing ladders and jumping around to apply color to a canvas. Solberg's process reminds me to step back from the work often and check in with the overall look. Knitting author Maggie Righetti echoes this approach, advising us to "stop often and admire our work." This is usually when I will notice a silly mistake or that something is not producing the desired effect. Stop, move, look, and, if needed, adjust.

Author and bon vivant **ANTHONY BOURDAIN** travels the globe in search of new food experiences. While he is known for his acerbic wit, I've always admired his observant, respectful way of being in the world. Wherever he lands, he is open and inquiring, absorbing everything from his surroundings and walking away improved. Nothing is beneath him, no meal or table too humble, and this omnivorous approach to life seems to yield unlimited joy. Adopt the same approach to art and fashion and see what happens.

SUBSTITUTING YARNS

WHEN IT COMES TO PAIRING A YARN WITH A PROJECT, THERE ARE TWO
SCHOOLS OF THOUGHT. THERE ARE THE KNITTERS WHO INSIST ON REPLICAT-
ING A SAMPLE GARMENT EXACTLY—THEY WILL BUY THE RECOMMENDED YARN
IN THE COLOR SHOWN, EVEN IF IT ISN'T A SHADE THEY PARTICULARLY CARE
FOR. THIS HAPPENS SO FREQUENTLY THAT SHOP OWNERS WILL OFTEN BUY
MORE OF A COLOR IF IT IS USED FOR A SAMPLE GARMENT, KNOWING THEY
WILL SELL OUT OF IT FIRST. I'LL SHARE A DIRTY LITTLE SECRET—I WILL OFTEN
CHOOSE A SLOW-MOVING COLOR FOR A SAMPLE GARMENT AND WATCH IN
DELIGHT AS IT SUDDENLY STARTS SELLING. THIS STRATEGY MIGHT BE RESPONSI-
BLE FOR THE RECENT POPULARITY OF MUSTARD AND CHARTREUSE—YELLOW IS
TRADITIONALLY A HARD SELL, AT LEAST IN NORTH AMERICA.

On the other end of the spectrum are the knitters who would never think of knitting a garment in exactly the same yarn and colorway shown. They view a pattern as a loose blueprint from which to riff. I respect this maverick attitude, as it tends to coincide with confidence and solid knitting skills. The knitters who purchase the "right" yarns may be doing so out of fear, believing erroneously that a pattern will only work if made with the yarn listed in the pattern. This is a common new-knitter impulse, but it is one that makes a lot of sense to me, considering the care and expertise that goes into yarn selection.

Being a primarily yarn-driven designer means that I never design a pattern without a yarn in mind. Often it's a specific yarn, but if it isn't, I still know the type of yarn I need to execute my design concept. This goes far beyond the usual substitution rubric, wherein you divide the per ball yardage of the new yarn, similar in weight, by the total yardage indicated for the original. Making sure you purchase the correct amount is only the first hurdle, and once cleared, you must make

sure you can get the gauge indicated in the pattern. On the surface, gauge refers to how many stitches and rows comprise an inch. It is the key number that governs the construction and execution of a garment, and the composition of its pattern. As all knitters know or must learn, gauge rules everything when it comes to garments. Garments and patterns live and die by gauge, and if you aren't careful about replicating it, you can kiss a proper fit good-bye.

The elusive last piece of the substitution puzzle is fabric. What does this mean? There is a recent trend of publishing patterns with actual measurements of both the garment shown and the model wearing it, plus the intended ease of the garment. Having information like this goes a long way toward making sure you can knit a garment with a fit that will please you. Similarly, knowing what the intended fabric is like will help you make your substitutions. Fiber is the first clue—think about the yarn listed, and the properties of all the fibers involved, and their construction. One-hundred-percent baby alpaca will behave entirely differently depending on how it is made—a dense two-ply may hang with a gloriously heavy drape, whereas a chainette construction can float and mimic the bounce of wool.

The second clue is gauge. I have been in the position of determining what goes on a ball band, that all-important road map to a specific ball of yarn. This means determining a needle size and a gauge but, truth be told, I hate committing this to paper! When I list a needle size and a gauge, know that it is merely a suggestion—a starting place. Ideally, I will indicate a range. My favorite yarns are the sort that can be knit to many gauges—more stitches per inch on a smaller needle size for a firm fabric that will stand up to lots of wear, or fewer stitches per inch on a larger needle for a soft and airy fabric. It's even possible to skew proportions by knitting worsted-weight yarns on outsized needles, rendering the medium-weight yarn lacy in the process. I utilize this trick often, manipulating fabric and gauge in projects like the Tisane Tank (page 70) and Meta Tee (page 74) without having to include dramatic shaping stitches.

In the beginning, my tendency was to knit yarns at a dense gauge. I loved the neatness of the stitches and the way my finished pieces seemed to be spring-loaded, like a Lycra-laced pair of skinny jeans. Somewhere along the line I realized that I was choking the life out of my yarn. Some yarns, especially single-plies and fuzzy fibers like angora or mohair, need room to breathe. Knit on a larger needle at a looser gauge, I discovered that what looks sloppy on the needles ends up fluid and soft after finishing. The yarns relax with a bit of heat and moisture, and the fibers fill in to create a gorgeous fabric. This is the sort of thing you learn from swatching and finishing your swatches. Finishing doesn't mean bind-off and go, I mean an actual blocking. Yes, it takes time, but it's the only way you can really get to know a yarn before committing to it fully.

This is all to say that gauge and fabric are the true test of whether a yarn will make an appropriate stand-in. My Aidez cardigan, which I designed for Berroco, has been knit by thousands of knitters and knitters don't usually use the yarn called for in the pattern. The yarn many of them use is quite a bit thinner than the original, and while they might be able to match the gauge, I know for certain that the feel of the fabric must be quite different. I knit the original in the spirit of a true Aran sweater, at a much firmer gauge than usual. My hands ached from knitting the thick, lofty fibers on needles smaller than what the ball band indicated, but I loved the stiff, traditional fabric, cables popping in high relief. The sweaters made with alternate yarns are completely serviceable garments, but something is lost in translation. This is, of course, up to the knitter to decide. To paraphrase a quote oft-credited to Voltaire (though there is some controversy surrounding its origin) I may disapprove of what you sub, but I will defend to the death your right to knit it. I hope you substitute with caution and confidence, taking the time to consider the suitability of any alternatives, remembering that swatching reveals all.

VENTURING INTO THE WORLD TO MEET FRIENDS AND GATHER INSPIRATION

NOMADS

WE'VE ESTABLISHED THAT KNITTERS LOVE TO SPEND TIME AT HOME AMONGST THEIR BEAUTIFUL OBJECTS, CREATING IN A WORLD OF THEIR OWN.

But this isn't the whole story. Knitters are just as mobile as they are sedentary; I am just as likely to be knitting on an airplane as I am to be knitting in an armchair. And thank goodness for that—my best ideas come from travel.

Any time spent away from familiar environs is a boon to developing a better sense of style. While it is all too easy to slip into a comfortable uniform at home, traveling requires a careful edit of your wardrobe—what will you pack to fit into this new locale? Beyond practical considerations about weather and situation, I find myself channeling the soul of that particular city. It could be pure conjecture, but it's still a worthwhile exercise. The baking heat and laidback attitude of Austin calls for cotton sundresses and colorful lace shawls worn as kerchiefs. A visit to Manhattan demands drama and strength; I default to black basics with a hard edge. Functionality is another key consideration. Deep pockets or securely fastening snaps instead of buttons (as on the Gezell Coat, page 98, and the Coterie Cardigan, page 92, respectively) serve me well when tromping around all day. Slippery shawls have no place in the commuter's wardrobe. Better to stick with a cowl or a hooded, sleeveless vest that will stay put under coats and not go missing.

When I do arrive, I keep my eyes wide open, taking stock of what the denizens of my temporary home are wearing. This is how I first noticed that young skaters on Bleecker Street were donning slouchy hats far back on their head—a look that would trickle up quickly to mainstream chain stores and knitters' needles alike. Visiting Iceland in March was a crash course in layering. Fur accents and cowls on top of enveloping sweaters weren't just quirky and eye-catching, they were necessary to guard against cutting winds.

Besides taking in the fashion show on the streets, I seize any opportunity to visit unique shops. Yarn stores are a natural default, but I also seek out one-off haberdasheries like Tender Buttons in New York City, a button store hardly bigger than a studio apartment but filled to the hilt with incredibly unique accents for knits. After I've had my fill of people-watching and shopping, I will usually find myself in a museum of some sort. In natural history museums I might be struck with a sweater idea after seeing a particularly interesting skeleton or fish gill. Traditional art museums often have a textile section, and I attack these voraciously, taking snapshots of my favorite pieces and sketching them when photography is banned. If I'm not feeling focused, I will revel in color, and most likely, other museumgoers. This is where I usually spot my favorite advanced fashionistas, and it makes sense: People who frequent museums tend to approach life as an art form, and clothing as just another medium.

COTERIE CARDIGAN

Coterie is a curve-hugging jacket with military lineage. Wry skull buttons give this trim cardigan a roguish edge, while slipped-stitch edges and twisted garter stitch keep it looking neat. The shapely silhouette worked in a sturdy, serviceable wool references uniforms that manage to combine beauty and utility.

SIZES

X-Small (Small, Medium, Large, 1X-Large, 2X-Large)

FINISHED MEASUREMENTS

33½ (37, 41¼, 46, 49½, 55)" [85 (94, 105, 117, 125.5, 139.5) cm] bust, buttoned

YARN

Cascade Ecological Wool [100% natural Peruvian wool; 478 yards (437 meters) / 250 grams]: 2 (3, 3, 3, 3, 4) hanks #8020 Gun Metal

NEEDLES

One 40" (100 cm) long circular (circ) needle size US 9 (5.5 mm)

One set of five double-pointed needles (dpn) size US 9 (5.5 mm)

Change needle size if necessary to obtain correct gauge.

NOTIONS

Stitch markers; stitch holders or waste yarn; ten 1" (25 mm) buttons; two 1" (25 mm) snaps (optional); sewing needle and thread (optional)

GAUGE

18 sts and 22 rows = 4" (10 cm) in Shadow Rib

18 sts and 28 rows = 4" (10 cm) in Twisted Garter Stitch Flat

NOTE

The Body is worked in one piece to the underarms, then Fronts and Back are worked separately to the shoulders. The Sleeves are worked from the bottom up, in the round.

STITCH PATTERNS

I-Cord Edging

(panel of 3 sts worked at beginning and end of row only)

ROW 1 (RS): At beginning of row, slip 3 sts purlwise; at end of row, k3.

ROW 2: At beginning of row, slip 3 sts purlwise; at end of row, p3.

Repeat Rows 1 and 2 for *I-Cord Edging.*

Shadow Rib Flat

(multiple of 3 sts + 2; 2-row repeat)

ROW 1 (RS): P2, *k1-tbl, p2; repeat from * to end.

ROW 2: Knit.

Repeat Rows 1 and 2 for *Shadow Rib Flat.*

Shadow Rib in the Round

(multiple of 3 sts; 2-rnd repeat)

RND 1: *P1, k1-tbl, p1; repeat from * to end.

RND 2: Purl.

Repeat Rnds 1 and 2 for *Shadow Rib in the Round.*

Twisted Garter Stitch Flat

(any number of sts; 1-row repeat)

ALL ROWS: *K1-tbl; repeat from * to end.

Twisted Garter Stitch in the Round

(any number of sts; 2-rnd repeat)

RND 1: *P1-tbl; repeat from * to end.

RND 2: *K1-tbl; repeat from * to end.

Repeat Rnds 1 and 2 for *Twisted Garter Stitch in the Round.*

SPECIAL TECHNIQUE

ONE-ROW BUTTONHOLE: Slip 1 wyif, bring yarn to back and leave it there (you won't use it while you are slipping sts), slip 1 wyib, pass first slipped st over second slipped st; [slip 1 wyib, pass slipped st over] 3 times; slip last slipped st back to left-hand needle, turn. Bring yarn to back; using Cable Cast-On Method (see Special Techniques, page 141), CO 5 sts, turn; wyib, slip st from left-hand needle back to right-hand needle; past last CO st over slipped st. Continue with row.

BODY

Using Long-Tail Cast-On (see Special Techniques, page 142), CO 189 (210, 228, 249, 270, 294) sts. Knit 4 rows.

NOTE: *Shadow Rib Flat is worked over 3 sections: Right Front, Back, and Left Front. Each section has a multiple of 3 sts + 2. Start each section over at the beginning of Shadow Rib Flat.*

ROW 1 (RS): Work I-Cord Edging over 3 sts, pm, work 53 (59, 62, 68, 74, 80) sts in Shadow Rib Flat, pm for side, work 77 (86, 98, 107, 116, 128) sts in Shadow Rib Flat, restarting pattern, pm for side, work 53 (59, 62, 68, 74, 80) sts in Shadow Rib Flat, restarting pattern, work I-Cord Edging over 3 sts.

Work even in patterns as established until piece measures 4 (4½, 5, 5½, 6, 6½)" [10 (11.5, 12.5, 14, 15, 16.5) cm] from the beginning, ending with a WS row.

SHAPE WAIST

NEXT ROW (RS): Continuing in patterns as established, decrease 4 sts this row, then every 6 rows 4 times, as follows: [Work to 3 sts before marker, ssk, k1, sm, k1, k2tog] twice, work to end—169 (190, 208, 229, 250, 274) sts remain. Work even until piece measures 9½ (10, 10¾, 11½, 12, 12½)" [24 (25.5, 27.5, 29, 30.5, 32) cm] from the beginning, ending with a WS row.

WORK WAISTBAND

NEXT ROW (RS): Continuing to work first and last 3 sts in I-Cord Edging, change to Twisted Garter Stitch Flat across remaining sts; work even for 11 rows.

NEXT ROW (WS): Continuing in patterns as established, work to marker, sm, work to next marker, decreasing 0 (1, 0, 0, 1, 0) st(s) or increasing 1 (0, 0, 1, 0, 0) st(s), sm, work to next marker, increasing 1 st, sm, work to next marker, decreasing 0 (1, 0, 0, 1, 0) st(s) or increasing 1 (0, 0, 1, 0, 0) st(s), sm, work to end—172 (189, 209, 232, 249, 275) sts.

NEXT ROW (RS): Work I-Cord Edging to marker, sm, work 26 (27, 28, 29, 30, 31) sts in Twisted Garter Stitch Flat, pm, work in Shadow Rib Flat to next marker, sm, work in Shadow Rib Flat, restarting pattern, to next marker, work in Shadow Rib Flat, restarting pattern, to last 29 (30, 31, 32, 33, 34) sts, pm, work Twisted Garter Stitch Flat to last 3 sts, work I-Cord Edging to end. Continuing to work in patterns as established, work even for 1½ (1¾, 1¾, 1¾, 1½, 1¾)" [4 (4.5, 4.5, 4.5, 4, 4.5) cm], ending with a WS row.

BUTTONHOLE ROW (RS): Work to marker, sm, work 3 (3, 3, 4, 4, 4) sts, work One-Row Buttonhole, work 12 (13, 14, 13, 14, 15) sts, work One-Row Buttonhole, work to end. Work even for 1 row.

SHAPE BUST

NEXT ROW (RS): Continuing to work in patterns as established, increase 4 sts this row, then every 6 rows once, working increased sts in Shadow Rib Flat as they become available, as follows: [Work to 1 st before side marker, M1-l, k1, sm, k1, M1-r] twice, work to end—180 (197, 217, 240, 257, 283) sts. Work even, working one additional Buttonhole Row 14 rows above previous Buttonhole Row, until piece measures 15¼ (15¾, 16½, 17¼, 17¾, 18¼)" [38.5 (40, 42, 44, 45, 46.5) cm] from the beginning, ending with a WS row.

DIVIDE FOR FRONTS AND BACK

NEXT ROW (RS): Work to 3 (6, 7, 8, 9, 10) sts before first side marker and place last 51 (52, 55, 61, 64, 70) sts worked on st holder or waste yarn for Right Front, BO next 6 (12, 14, 16, 18, 20) sts, removing marker, work to 3 (6, 7, 8, 9, 10) sts before next side marker and place last 66 (69, 79, 86, 93, 103) sts worked on st holder or waste yarn for Back, BO next 6 (12, 14, 16, 18, 20) sts, removing marker, work to end.

LEFT FRONT

Working on 51 (52, 55, 61, 64, 70) Left Front sts only, work even for 1 row.

SHAPE ARMHOLE

NEXT ROW (RS): Continuing to work in patterns as established, BO 2 sts at armhole edge 0 (0, 0, 2, 2, 4) times, then decrease 1 st at armhole edge every other row 2 (3, 5, 4, 6, 5) times, as follows: K1, k2tog, work to end—49 (49, 50, 53, 54, 57) sts remain. Work even until armhole measures 6¼ (6½, 7, 7¼, 7¼, 7½)" [16 (16.5, 18, 18.5, 18.5, 19) cm], ending with a RS row.

SHAPE NECK

NEXT ROW (WS): [P2, p2tog, slip sts back to left-hand needle] 26 (27, 28, 29, 30, 31) times, work to end—23 (22, 22, 24, 24, 26) sts remain. Work even for 1 row.

NEXT ROW (WS): [P2, p2tog, slip sts back to left-hand needle] twice, work to end—21 (20, 20, 22, 22, 24) sts remain. Work even, working 3 sts at neck edge in I-Cord Edging, until armhole measures 7¾ (8, 8½, 8¾, 9¼, 9½)" [19.5 (20.5, 21.5, 22, 23.5, 24) cm], ending with a WS row.

SHAPE SHOULDER

NEXT ROW (RS): BO 6 (6, 6, 6, 6, 7) sts at armhole edge twice, then 6 (5, 5, 7, 7, 7) sts once. Place remaining 3 sts on st holder for Back neckband.

BACK

With WS facing, rejoin yarn to sts on st holder for Back.

SHAPE ARMHOLES

NEXT ROW (WS): BO 2 sts at beginning of next 0 (0, 0, 4, 4, 8) rows, then decrease 1 st each side every other row 2 (3, 5, 4, 6, 5) times, as follows: K1, k2tog, work to last 3 sts, ssk, k1—62 (63, 69, 70, 73, 77) sts remain. Work even until armholes measure 7¾ (8, 8½, 8¾, 9¼, 9½)" [19.5 (20.5, 21.5, 22, 23.5, 24) cm], ending with a WS row.

SHAPE SHOULDERS

NEXT ROW (RS): BO 6 (6, 6, 6, 6, 7) sts at beginning of next 4 rows, then 6 (5, 5, 7, 7, 7) sts at beginning of next 2 rows. Place remaining 26 (29, 35, 32, 35, 35) sts on st holder for Back neck.

RIGHT FRONT

With WS facing, rejoin yarn to sts on st holder for Right Front.

SHAPE ARMHOLE

NEXT ROW (WS): Continuing to work in patterns as established, and working an additional Buttonhole Row 14 rows above previous Buttonhole Row if necessary, BO 2 sts at armhole edge 0 (0, 0, 2, 2, 4) times, then decrease 1 st at armhole edge every other row 2 (3, 5, 4, 6, 5) times, as follows: Work to last 3 sts, k2tog, k1—49 (49, 50, 53, 54, 57) sts remain. Continuing to work additional Buttonhole Rows 14 rows above the previous Buttonhole Row until you have a total of 5 Buttonhole Rows, work until armhole measures 6¼ (6½, 6¾, 7, 6¾, 7)" [16 (16.5, 17, 18, 17, 18) cm], ending with a WS row.

SHAPE NECK

NEXT ROW (RS): [K2, ssk, slip sts back to left-hand needle] 26 (27, 28, 29, 30, 31) times, work to end—23 (22, 22, 24, 24, 26) sts remain. Work even for 1 row.

NEXT ROW (RS): [K2, ssk, slip sts back to left-hand needle] twice, work to end—21 (20, 20, 22, 22, 24) sts remain. Work even, working 3 sts at neck edge in I-Cord Edging, until armhole measures 7¾ (8, 8½, 8¾, 9¼, 9½)" [19.5 (20.5, 21.5, 22, 23.5, 24) cm], ending with a RS row.

SHAPE SHOULDER

NEXT ROW (WS): BO 6 (6, 6, 6, 6, 7) sts at armhole edge twice, then 6 (5, 5, 7, 7, 7) sts once. Place remaining 3 sts on st holder for Back neckband.

SLEEVES

Using dpns and Long-Tail Cast-On (see Special Techniques, page 142), CO 42 (42, 45, 48, 51, 51) sts. Join for working in the rnd, being careful not to twist sts; pm for beginning of rnd. Begin Twisted Garter Stitch in the Round; work even until piece measures 3" (7.5 cm) from the beginning.

NEXT RND: Change to Shadow Rib in the Round; work even for 2 rnds.

SHAPE SLEEVE

NEXT RND: Increase 2 sts this rnd, then every 9 (6, 7, 4, 4, 3) rnds 2 (3, 4, 7, 8, 12) times, working increased sts into pattern as they become available, as follows: Work 2 sts, M1-l, work to last 2 sts, M1-r, work 2 sts —48 (50, 55, 64, 69, 77) sts. Work even until piece measures 9 (9, 10, 10, 10½, 10½)" [23 (23, 25.5, 25.5, 26.5, 26.5) cm] from the beginning, ending 3 (6, 7, 8, 9, 10) sts before end of final rnd.

SHAPE CAP

NEXT RND: BO 6 (12, 14, 16, 18, 20) sts—42 (38, 41, 48, 51, 57) sts remain. Work even for 1 row.

NEXT RND (RS): Decrease 1 st each side this row, every other row 4 (0, 1, 6, 8, 12) time(s), then every 4 rows 5 (7, 7, 5, 4, 2) time(s), as follows: K1, k2tog, work to last 3 sts, ssk, k1. BO 3 sts at beginning of next 4 rows. BO remaining 10 (10, 11, 12, 13, 15) sts.

FINISHING

Sew shoulder seams.

BACK NECKBAND

Transfer Back neck sts to circ needle; transfer 3 Right Front sts to right-hand end of circ needle, in front of Back neck sts—29 (32, 38, 35, 38, 38) sts. *K2, ssk, do not turn, slip sts back to left-hand needle; repeat from *, pulling yarn from left to right for first st, until 3 sts remain. Using Kitchener st, graft sts to 3 sts from Left Front.

Set in Sleeves. Sew on buttons opposite buttonholes. Sew snaps to WS of Right Front and RS of Left Front, next to top two buttons and buttonholes, for additional security (optional).

Block as desired.

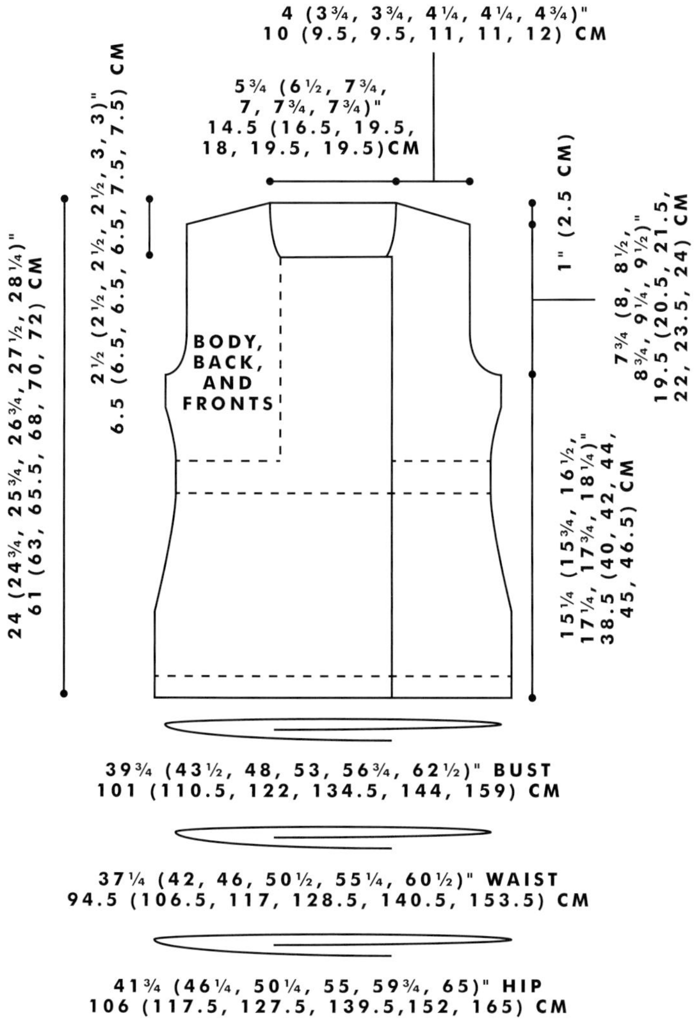
4 (3¾, 3¾, 4¼, 4¼, 4¾)"
10 (9.5, 9.5, 11, 11, 12) CM
5¾ (6½, 7¾, 7, 7¾, 7¾)"
14.5 (16.5, 19.5, 18, 19.5, 19.5)CM
2½ (2½, 2½, 2½, 3, 3)"
6.5 (6.5, 6.5, 6.5, 7.5, 7.5) CM
24 (24¾, 25¾, 26¾, 27½, 28¼)"
61 (63, 65.5, 68, 70, 72) CM
1" (2.5 CM)
7¾ (8, 8½, 8¾, 9¼, 9½)"
19.5 (20.5, 21.5, 22, 23.5, 24) CM
15¼ (15¾, 16½, 17¼, 17¾, 18¼)"
38.5 (40, 42, 44, 45, 46.5) CM
BODY, BACK, AND FRONTS
39¾ (43½, 48, 53, 56¾, 62½)" BUST
101 (110.5, 122, 134.5, 144, 159) CM
37¼ (42, 46, 50½, 55¼, 60½)" WAIST
94.5 (106.5, 117, 128.5, 140.5, 153.5) CM
41¾ (46¼, 50¼, 55, 59¾, 65)" HIP
106 (117.5, 127.5, 139.5,152, 165) CM

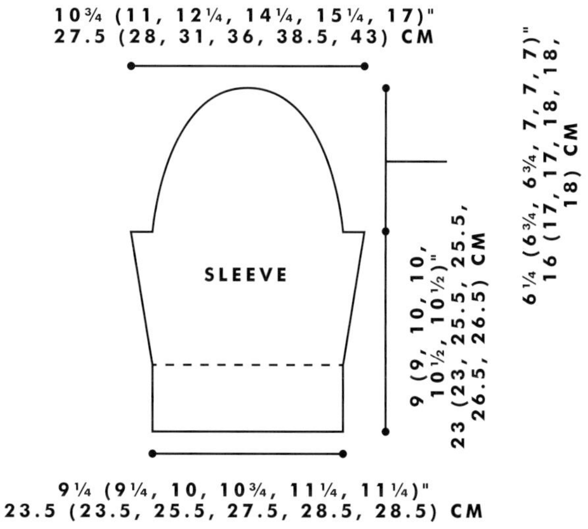
10¾ (11, 12¼, 14¼, 15¼, 17)"
27.5 (28, 31, 36, 38.5, 43) CM
6¼ (6¾, 6¾, 7, 7, 7)"
16 (17, 17, 18, 18, 18) CM
SLEEVE
9 (9, 10, 10, 10½, 10½)"
23 (23, 25.5, 25.5, 26.5, 26.5) CM
9¼ (9¼, 10, 10¾, 11¼, 11¼)"
23.5 (23.5, 25.5, 27.5, 28.5, 28.5) CM

GEZELL COAT

Pockets seem to be a universally loved feature, and it's easy to see why, but adding them to handknit sweaters can be a bit problematic. Patch pockets are cute, but often awkwardly placed, and adding side pockets to a form-fitting garment can create unsightly bulk. I circumvented these issues by knitting two mirrored halves with afterthought pockets situated right where hands naturally fall.

The loose cocoon shape hides any bulges that might result from the pocket linings, while three-quarter-length sleeves keep the generous silhouette from overwhelming the wearer. An exposed seam in back is flanked by decorative eyelet increases, while tight bobbles adorn hem and sleeve edges. The yarn is a surprising technical wonder; what looks like a single ply is actually a fine silk tube that holds fluffy baby alpaca fiber. It is light, incomparably soft, and pill-resistant.

SIZES
Small (Medium, Large)

FINISHED MEASUREMENTS
51½ (58½, 67½)" [131 (148.5, 171.5) cm] bust

YARN
Schulana Royalpaca [78% royal alpaca / 22% silk; 120 yards (109.5 meters) / 50 grams]: 10 (12, 13) balls #06 Pitch Black

NEEDLES
One 16" (40 cm) long circular (circ) needle size US 8 (5 mm)

One 16" (40 cm) long circular needle size US 9 (5.5 mm)

One 24" (60 cm) long circular needle size US 8 (5 mm)

One 24" (60 cm) long circular (circ) needle size US 9 (5.5 mm)

One set of five double-pointed needles (dpn) size US 8 (5 mm)

Change needle size if necessary to obtain correct gauge.

NOTIONS
Waste yarn; stitch marker

GAUGE
14 sts and 20 rows = 4" (10 cm) in Stockinette stitch (St st), using larger needles

ABBREVIATION
MB (Make Bobble): Knit into front, back, then front of next st to increase to 3 sts, turn; p3, turn; k3tog to decrease to 1 st.

NOTE
The Body of the Coat is worked back and forth in two symmetrical pieces, the Right Front/Back and Left Front/Back, which are then sewn together at the center back. The Sleeves are picked up from the armholes and worked in the round to the cuff.

STITCH PATTERNS

Bobble Rib Flat

(multiple of 4 sts + 3; 2-row repeat)

ROW 1 (RS): *K3, p1; repeat from * to last 3 sts, k3.

ROW 2: *P3, k1; repeat from * to last 3 sts, p3.

Repeat Rows 1 and 2 for 2" (5 cm), ending with Row 2.

BOBBLE ROW (RS): *K1, MB, k1, p1; repeat from * to last 3 sts, k1, MB, k1.

Repeat Row 2, then repeat Rows 1 and 2 for ½" (1.5 cm), ending with Row 2.

Bobble Rib in the Round

(multiple of 4 sts; 1-rnd repeat)

RND 1: *K3, p1; repeat from * to end.

Repeat Rnd 1 once.

BOBBLE RND: *K1, MB, k1, p1; rep from * to end.

Repeat Rnd 1 twice.

1x1 Rib

(odd number of sts; 2-row repeat)

ROW 1 (RS): Slip 1 purlwise, *k1, p1; repeat from * to last 2 sts, k2.

ROW 2: P2, *k1, p1; repeat from * to last st, p1.

Repeat Rows 1 and 2 for *1x1 Rib.*

LEFT FRONT/BACK

Using smaller 24" (60 cm) circ needle, CO 73 (85, 101) sts.

NEXT ROW (RS): K1 (edge st, keep in St st), work Bobble Rib Flat to last st, k1 (edge st, keep in St st). Work even until Bobble Rib Flat is complete. Place marker 26 (32, 40) sts in from right-hand edge.

SHAPE BODY AND WORK POCKET OPENING

NOTE: *Body shaping and Pocket Opening are worked at the same time; please read entire section through before beginning.*

NEXT ROW (RS): Change to larger needle. Increase 1 st each side this row, then every 8 rows 4 times, as follows: K2, yo, knit last 2 sts, yo, k2—83 (95, 111) sts. AT THE SAME TIME, when piece measures 7½" (19 cm) from the beginning, shape Pocket Opening as follows:

NEXT ROW (RS): Continuing to work body shaping as established, work to marker, remove marker, change to waste yarn, k21, slide these 21 sts back to left-hand needle, change to working yarn, knit these 21 sts again, work to end. When body shaping is complete, work even for 7 rows.

NEXT ROW (RS): K2, yo, k2tog, knit to last 4 sts, ssk, yo, k2. Repeat last row every 8 rows 4 times. Work even for 7 rows.

DIVIDE FOR BACK AND FRONT

NEXT ROW (RS): K2, yo, k2tog, k27 (33, 41), place last 31 (37, 45) sts worked on waste yarn for Back, k21 and place these sts on separate waste yarn for underarm, knit to end (discontinuing [ssk, yo, k2] at end of every 8 rows)—31 (37, 45) sts remain for Front.

FRONT

Working on Front sts only, purl 1 row.

SHAPE ARMHOLE AND NECK

NOTE: *Armhole and neck are shaped at the same time; please read entire section through before beginning.*

NEXT ROW (RS): Decrease 1 st at armhole edge this row, then every 8 rows 3 times, as follows: K1, ssk, knit to end. AT THE SAME TIME, beginning on first row of armhole shaping, begin neck shaping as follows:

NEXT ROW (RS): Decrease 1 st at neck edge this row, then every 4 rows 7 times, as follows: Work to last 3 sts, k2tog, k1—19 (25, 33) sts remain after all shaping is complete. Work even until armhole measures 7" (18 cm), ending with a WS row.

SHAPE SHOULDER

NEXT ROW (RS): BO 5 (6, 8) sts at armhole edge 3 times, then 4 (7, 9) sts once.

BACK

With WS facing, rejoin yarn to Back sts. Purl 1 row.

SHAPE ARMHOLE

NEXT ROW (RS): Continuing to work [k2, yo, k2tog] at beginning of row every 8 rows as established, decrease 1 st at armhole edge this row, then every 8 rows 3 times, as follows: Knit to last 3 sts, k2tog, k1—27 (33, 41) sts remain. Continuing to work [k2, yo, k2tog] at beginning of every 8 rows as established, work even until armhole measures 7" (18 cm), ending with a RS row.

SHAPE SHOULDER

NEXT ROW (WS): BO 5 (6, 8) sts at armhole edge 3 times, 4 (7, 9) sts once, then 8 sts once.

RIGHT FRONT/BACK

Work as for Left Back/Front to divide for Front and Back.

DIVIDE FOR BACK AND FRONT

NEXT ROW (RS): K31 (37, 45) (discontinuing [k2, yo, k2tog] at beginning of every 8 rows) and place these sts on waste yarn for Front, k21 and place these sts on separate waste yarn for underarm, knit to last 4 sts, ssk, yo, k2—31 (37, 45) sts remain for Back.

BACK

Working on Back sts only, purl 1 row.

SHAPE ARMHOLE

NEXT ROW (RS): Continuing to work [ssk, yo, k2] at end of row every 8 rows as established, decrease 1 st at armhole edge this row, then every 8 rows 3 times, as follows: K1, ssk, work to end—27 (33, 41) sts remain. Continuing to work [ssk, yo, k2] at end of every 8 rows as established, work even until armhole measures 7" (18 cm), ending with a WS row.

SHAPE SHOULDER

NEXT ROW (RS): BO 5 (6, 8) sts at armhole edge 3 times, 4 (7, 9) sts once, then 8 sts once.

FRONT

With WS facing, rejoin yarn to Front sts. Purl 1 row.

SHAPE ARMHOLE AND NECK

NOTE: *Armhole and neck are shaped at the same time; please read entire section through before beginning.*

NEXT ROW (RS): Decrease 1 st at armhole edge this row, then every 8 rows 3 times, as follows: Knit to last 3 sts, k2tog, k1. AT THE SAME TIME, beginning on first row of armhole shaping, begin neck shaping as follows:

NEXT ROW (RS): Decrease 1 st at neck edge this row, then every 4 rows 7 times, as follows: K1, ssk, work to end—19 (25, 33) sts remain after all shaping is complete. Work even until armhole measures 7" (18 cm), ending with a WS row.

SHAPE SHOULDER

Next Row (WS): BO 5 (6, 8) sts at armhole edge 3 times, then 4 (7, 9) sts once.

SLEEVES

Fold each Front/Back in half widthwise. Sew shoulder seams, leaving last 8 sts of each Back unsewn (for Back neck). With RSs together (WSs facing), sew Back halves of Left and Right Front/Back together (seam will be visible on RS), making sure to align eyelets as you sew. Transfer 21 underarm sts from waste yarn to right-hand end of larger 24" (60 cm) circ needle. Working across these sts, k11, pm for beginning of rnd, k10, pick up and knit 57 sts around armhole edge to sts from waste yarn, knit to marker—78 sts. Begin St st (knit every rnd); work even for 4 rnds.

SHAPE SLEEVE

NOTE: *Change to larger 16" (40 cm) circ needle as necessary for number of sts on needle.*

NEXT RND: Decrease 2 sts this rnd, then every 5 rnds 10 times, as follows: K2, ssk, knit to last 5 sts before marker, k2tog, k3—56 sts remain. Work even until piece measures 11" (28 cm) from pick-up rnd.

NEXT RND: Change to smaller 16" (40 cm) circ needle and Bobble Rib in the Round; work even until Rib is complete.

NEXT RND: Change to smaller dpns. *K2tog, k1, p1; repeat from * to end—42 sts remain. BO all sts in Rib.

FINISHING

Pocket Lining

Carefully remove waste yarn from Pocket Opening sts and place bottom 21 and top 20 sts onto 2 smaller dpns, being careful not to twist sts. With RS facing, rejoin yarn to bottom sts, pick up and knit 1 st at side of Pocket Opening, knit across 21 bottom sts, pick up and knit 1 st at other side of Pocket Opening, knit across 20 top sts— 43 sts. Redistribute sts among 3 dpns. Join for working in the rnd; pm for beginning of rnd. Continuing in St st, work even until piece measures 6" (15 cm), or to desired length from pick-up rnd, decreasing 1 bottom st on final rnd—42 sts remain. Place bottom sts on one dpn, and top sts on a second. Push Pocket Lining through Pocket Opening, so that Lining is now on inside of Coat, and needles are to outside (purl side) of Lining. Using Three-Needle BO, join bottom and top sts.

Neckband

Using smaller dpns, CO 15 sts. Begin 1x1 Rib; work even until piece measures 57¾" (146.5 cm), or long enough to fit around entire Front and Back neck edge, slightly stretched; leave sts on needle. Sew Neckband to Fronts and Back neck, making sure slipped edge is the exposed edge, and sewing approximately 2 Neckband rows to every 3 Front rows; take out rows or work additional rows if necessary to make Neckband fit without bunching. BO all sts in Rib.

Block as desired.

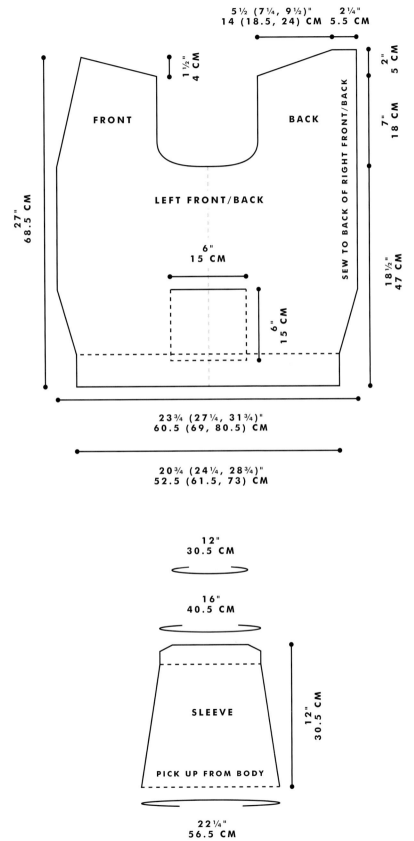

5 ½ (7 ¼, 9 ½)"   2 ¼"
14 (18.5, 24) CM   5.5 CM

1 ½"
4 CM

2"
5 CM

7"
18 CM

FRONT

BACK

SEW TO BACK OF RIGHT FRONT/BACK

27"
68.5 CM

LEFT FRONT/BACK

18 ½"
47 CM

6"
15 CM

6"
15 CM

23 ¾ (27 ¼, 31 ¾)"
60.5 (69, 80.5) CM

20 ¾ (24 ¼, 28 ¾)"
52.5 (61.5, 73) CM

12"
30.5 CM

16"
40.5 CM

12"
30.5 CM

SLEEVE

PICK UP FROM BODY

22 ¼"
56.5 CM

JORDAAN CAPE

The Jordaan Cape is an example of how important it is to literally shop for inspiration. I was browsing an indie boutique in the Jordaan district of Amsterdam, a cool little enclave filled with colorful cosmetics boutiques and craft-focused ateliers. A faux cow print cocoon jumped off the shelf and at first, baffled me. Flared at the bottom with a striking stand-up bateau collar, the dramatic piece looked like a skirt, but closer inspection revealed two horizontal slits near the lower hemline.

The charming boutique owner informed me that the piece was actually a playful take on a poncho. I bought it, but truth be told, I'm still trying to figure out where one should wear a cow-print poncho! No matter, it lives in my workshop alongside other odd, never-worn garments purchased purely for their ability to send my imagination reeling. The Jordaan Cape is an abbreviated version of my fantastical bovine poncho—hopefully a more wearable incarnation.

SIZES

Small (Medium, Large, 1X-Large, 2X-Large)

FINISHED MEASUREMENTS

38 (42½, 46, 50½, 54)" [96.5 (108, 117, 128.5, 137) cm] at widest point, after cutting steek

YARN

Peace Fleece Worsted Weight [75% wool / 25% mohair; 200 yards (183 meters) / 4 ounces (113 grams)]: 3 (4, 4, 5, 5) hanks Father's Gray (MC)

Sirri Sirritógv Colour [100% wool; 229 yards (209.5 meters) / 100 grams]: 1 hank #C3 (A)

Note: Because this pattern uses a steek, it is essential to use "sticky" pure wool yarn that will help to keep the steeks from unraveling.

NEEDLES

One 40" (100 cm) long circular (circ) needle size US 10 (6 mm)

One 12" (30 cm) long [16" (40 cm) long for last 3 sizes] circular needle size US 10 (6 mm)

One set of five double-pointed needles (dpns) size US 9 (5.5 mm)

One 16" (40 cm) long circular needle size US 9 (5.5 mm)

Change needle size if necessary to obtain correct gauge.

NOTIONS

Crochet hook size US G/6 (4 mm); stitch marker; waste yarn; sharp scissors; 52 (54, 56, 58, 60)" [132 (137, 142, 147.5, 152.5) cm] long 1" (2.5 cm) wide cotton tape or grosgrain ribbon; sewing thread and needle; large hook and eye closure

GAUGE

14 sts and 22 rows = 4" (10 cm) in Stockinette stitch (St st), using larger needle and 1 strand of MC

NOTE

The Cape is worked in the round with a steek up the center front. The sides of the steek are reinforced with single crochet, then the steek is cut and the cut ends are covered with cotton tape or a grosgrain ribbon to secure the stitches. Arm slits are worked in waste yarn, then unraveled and worked in a contrast yarn.

STITCH PATTERNS

Seeded Rib in the Round

(odd number of sts; 2-rnd repeat)

RND 1: *K1, p1; repeat from * to last st, k1.

RND 2: Knit.

Repeat Rnds 1 and 2 for *Seeded Rib in the Round.*

Seeded Rib Flat

(odd number of sts; 2-row repeat)

ROW 1: Knit.

RND 2: *P1, k1; repeat from * to last st, p1.

Repeat Rows 1 and 2 for *Seeded Rib Flat.*

BODY

Using 40" (100 cm) long circ needle and 2 strands of A held together, CO 138 (154, 166, 182, 194) sts. Join for working in the rnd, being careful not to twist sts; pm for beginning of rnd. K5 (steek sts), pm for end of steek, purl to end.

NEXT RND: Change to 1 strand of MC; knit to marker, work in Seeded Rib in the Round to end. Work even, keeping first 5 sts in St st, and remaining sts in Seeded Rib in the Round, until piece measures 5½" (14 cm) from the beginning.

NEXT RND: Change to St st across all sts; work even until piece measures 7½" (19 cm) from the beginning.

SHAPE ARM SLITS

NEXT RND: K16, *change to waste yarn, k18 (20, 20, 22, 22), slip these 18 (20, 20, 22, 22) sts back to left-hand needle, change to working yarn, knit these 18 (20, 20, 22, 22) sts again*, knit to last 29 (31, 31, 33, 33) sts, repeat from * to * once, knit to end. Work even until piece measures 17 (17¾, 18¾, 19¾, 20½)" [43 (45, 47.5, 50, 52) cm] from the beginning.

YOKE

SHAPE YOKE

NOTE: *Change to shorter circ needle when necessary for number of sts on the needle.*

DECREASE RND 1: Knit to marker, *k2, k2tog; repeat from * to last st, k1—105 (117, 126, 138, 147) sts remain. Work even until piece measures 18¼ (19¼, 20, 21¼, 22)" [46.5 (49, 51, 54, 56) cm] from the beginning.

DECREASE RND 2: Knit to marker, *k1, k2tog; repeat from * to last st, k1—72 (80, 86, 94, 100) sts remain. Work even until piece measures 19 (20, 21, 22, 23)" [48.5 (51, 53.5, 56, 58.5) cm] from the beginning.

DECREASE RND 3: Knit to marker, *k1, [k2tog] twice; repeat from * to last 2 (0, 1, 4, 0) st(s), knit to end—46 (50, 54, 60, 62) sts remain. Work even for 1 rnd.

COLLAR

NEXT ROW (RS): Change to working back and forth. BO 5 steek sts, work in Seeded Rib Flat to end—41 (45, 49, 55, 57) sts remain.

NOTE: *The st that remains on right-hand needle after BO will be considered the first st of Seeded Rib.*

Work even until piece measures 3½" (9 cm) from beginning of Seeded Rib, ending with a WS row.

NEXT ROW (RS): Change to 2 strands of A held together. Knit 1 row, knit 1 row (Turning Row).

NEXT ROW (RS): Change to smaller circ needle and St st; work even until piece measures 3" (7.5 cm) from color change, ending with a RS row.

NEXT ROW (WS): Change to MC; purl 1 row. BO all sts knitwise. Cut yarn, leaving a 24" (61 cm) tail.

FINISHING

CUT STEEK

With RS facing, beginning at lower edge, and using crochet hook and MC, anchor yarn in CO edge just to left of middle steek st by working 1 single crochet st into CO edge. Working into first st in knit column to left of middle steek st, *insert crochet hook under both legs of st, draw up a loop (2 sts on hook), yo hook, and pull loop through both sts on hook; repeat from * along entire column, working final st into BO edge, fasten off. Repeat for knit column on opposite side of middle steek st, beginning at BO edge and working toward CO edge. Working from the RS, using sharp scissors, cut into center of center steek st, between crocheted columns, working exactly in middle of st. When steek is cut, using sewing needle and thread, sew cotton tape or grosgrain ribbon over loose ends of cut steek on WS, being careful not to let sts show on RS.

COLLAR

Fold BO edge to WS at Turning Row and sew BO edge to WS, being careful not to let sts show on RS; sew side edges of Collar closed. Sew halves of hook and eye closure to WS at base of Collar.

ARM SLIT EDGING

Carefully remove waste yarn from Arm Slits and place bottom 18 (20, 20, 22, 22) sts and top 17 (19, 19, 21, 21) sts onto 2 dpns, being careful not to twist sts. With RS facing, using 2 strands of A held together, rejoin yarn to bottom sts, pick up and knit 1 st at side of Arm Slit, knit across 18 (20, 20, 22, 22) bottom sts, pick up and knit 1 st at other side of Arm Slit, knit across 17 (19, 19, 21, 21) top sts—37 (41, 41, 45, 45) sts. Purl 1 rnd. BO all sts.

Block as desired.

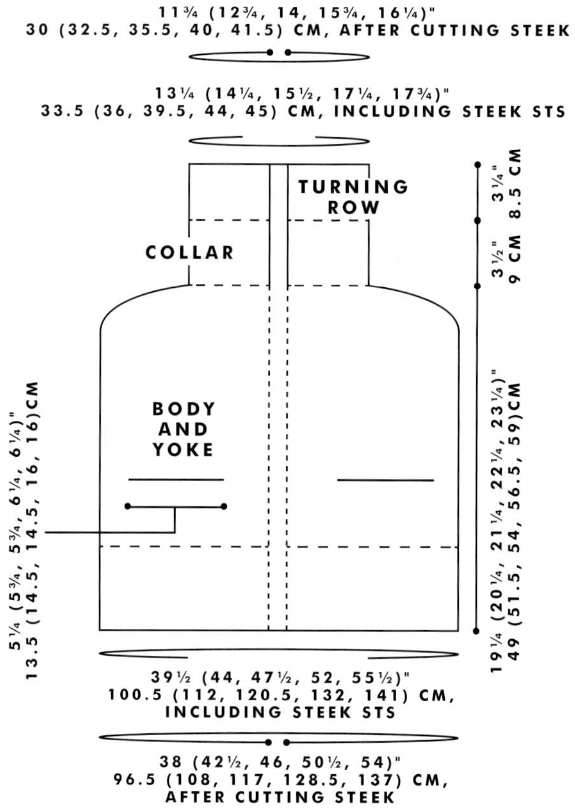
11¾ (12¾, 14, 15¾, 16¼)"
30 (32.5, 35.5, 40, 41.5) CM, AFTER CUTTING STEEK
13¼ (14¼, 15½, 17¼, 17¾)"
33.5 (36, 39.5, 44, 45) CM, INCLUDING STEEK STS
TURNING ROW
COLLAR
3¼" 8.5 CM
3½" 9 CM
BODY AND YOKE
5¼ (5¾, 5¾, 6¼, 6¼)"
13.5 (14.5, 14.5, 16, 16)CM
19¼ (20¼, 21¼, 22¼, 23¼)"
49 (51.5, 54, 56.5, 59)CM
39½ (44, 47½, 52, 55½)"
100.5 (112, 120.5, 132, 141) CM, INCLUDING STEEK STS
38 (42½, 46, 50½, 54)"
96.5 (108, 117, 128.5, 137) CM, AFTER CUTTING STEEK

LEVITT HAT

Levitt is an exercise in simplicity. Marled, handspun cashmere is a delightful portmanteau of woodsy charm and luxurious softness, and it doesn't require much in the way of stitch patterning. With yarns this special, I find it best to exercise restraint. Swatching usually confirms this hunch. A simple band of seed stitch breaks up the slouchy beanie, knit in a striking, classic palette that works in the woods or downtown.

FINISHED MEASUREMENTS
21¼" (54 cm) circumference

YARN
Jade Sapphire Exotic Fibers Handspun Cashmere [100% Mongolian cashmere; 120 yards (109.5 meters) / 50 grams]: 1 hank each Orca (MC) and Coral Reef (A)

NEEDLES
One 16" (40 cm) long circular (circ) needle size US 5 (3.75 mm)

One 16" (40 cm) long circular needle size US 6 (4 mm)

One set of five double-pointed needles (dpn) size US 6 (4 mm)

Change needle size if necessary to obtain correct gauge.

NOTIONS
Stitch marker

GAUGE
18 sts and 24 rows = 4" (10 cm) in Stockinette stitch (St st), using larger needles

STITCH PATTERNS

1x1 Rib
(even number of sts; 1-rnd repeat)
ALL RNDS: *K1, p1; repeat from * to end.

Seed Stitch
(odd number of sts; 2-rnd repeat)
RND 1: P1, *k1, p1; repeat from * to end.
RND 2: K1, *p1, k1; repeat from * to end.
Repeat Rnds 1 and 2 for *Seed Stitch*.

HAT

Using smaller needle and MC, CO 96 sts. Join for working in the rnd, being careful not to twist sts; pm for beginning of rnd. Begin 1x1 Rib; work even until piece measures 1" (2.5 cm) from the beginning.

NEXT RND: Change to larger circular needle and St st (knit every rnd); work even until piece measures 2½" (6.5 cm) from the beginning, decreasing 1 st at end of last rnd—95 sts remain.

NEXT RND: Change to A; slip 1 wyib, *p1, slip 1 wyib; repeat from * to end.

NEXT RND: Change to Seed st; work even until piece measures 4" (10 cm) from the beginning, ending with Rnd 2.

NEXT RND: Change to MC; slip 1 wyib, *p1, slip 1 wyib; repeat from * to end.

NEXT RND: Change to St st; work even until piece measures 7½" (19 cm) from the beginning, increasing 1 st at beginning of first rnd—96 sts.

SHAPE CROWN

NOTE: *Change to dpns when necessary for number of sts on needle.*

RND 1: *K4, k2tog; repeat from * to end—80 sts remain.

RNDS 2, 4, 6, AND 8: Knit.

RND 3: *K3, k2tog; repeat from * to end—64 sts remain.

RND 5: *K2, k2tog; repeat from * to end—48 sts remain.

RND 7: *K1, k2tog; repeat from * to end—32 sts remain.

RND 9: *K2tog; repeat from * to end—16 sts remain.

RND 10: Repeat Rnd 9—8 sts remain.

Cut yarn, leaving a 12" (30.5 cm) tail. Thread tail through remaining sts, pull tight, and fasten off.

FINISHING

Block as desired.

RAINIER COWL

Suede leather and shearling are natural partners. The soft, matte skin backed by the cozy natural texture of sheep fleece made a captivating choice for Tom Hardy's Bane costume in Christopher Nolan's *Dark Knight Rises*. The villain's dramatic full-length coat was tough and worn on the outside, but the scuffed patina reversed to a soft interior, a costuming choice that brilliantly captured his character arc. This cowl is an homage to that contrast. Plush, Aran-weight merino looks crisp in a simple offset rib pattern while sumptuous novelty yarn in off-white serves as a perfect stand-in for shearling lining. I often find my eyes darting around at the cinema, taking in every detail of a set or costume, missing the plot entirely. Thank goodness for Netflix….

FINISHED MEASUREMENTS
Approximately 24" (61 cm) circumference x 14" (35.5 cm) tall

YARN
HiKoo Simpliworsted [55% merino superwash / 28% acrylic / 17% nylon; 140 yards (128 meters) / 100 grams]: 2 hanks #064 Totally Taupe (A)

HiKoo Caribou [100% nylon; 93 yards (85 meters) / 50 grams]: 2 balls #003 Natural (B)

NEEDLES
One 24" (60 cm) long circular (circ) needle size US 9 (5.5 mm)

One spare 20" (50 cm) long or longer circular needle size US 9 (5.5 mm), for Kitchener st

Change needle size if necessary to obtain correct gauge.

NOTIONS
Crochet hook size US J/10 (6 mm); waste yarn; stitch marker; tapestry needle

GAUGE
16 sts and 21 rows = 4" (10 cm) in Offset Rib, using A

STITCH PATTERN
Offset Rib
(multiple of 4 sts; 18-rnd repeat)
RNDS 1–9: *K3, p1; repeat from * to end.
RNDS 10–18: *P1, k1, p2; repeat from * to end.
Repeat Rnds 1–18 for *Offset Rib*.

COWL

Using crochet hook, waste yarn, and Provisional (Crochet Chain) CO (see Special Techniques, page 142), CO 116 sts. Change to A. Join for working in the rnd, being careful not to twist sts; pm for beginning of rnd. Knit 1 rnd.

NEXT RND: Change to Offset Rib; work even until piece measures approximately 14" (35.5 cm) from the beginning, ending with Rnd 9 or 18 of pattern. Knit 1 rnd; cut yarn.

NEXT RND: Change to B and St st (knit every rnd); work even until piece measures 26" (66 cm) from the beginning; cut yarn. Change to A; knit 1 rnd.

FINISHING

With RS facing, carefully unravel Provisional CO and place sts on spare needle. Fold Cowl in half at beginning of B and, using Kitchener st (see Special Techniques, page 141), graft live sts to sts from Provisional CO. Block as desired.

RAVEN BAG

Many of my best ideas arrive fully formed, which never fails to astonish me. As much as I might wrestle through other things, or gather ideas to cobble together in a garment, my favorite and most successful items seem to be the product of some kind of spiritual divination. In the case of the Raven Bag, I knew that I wanted to design a cross-body purse using Berroco Lustra, an intriguing merino and Tencel blend that I actually prefer felted. The shiny plant fiber is trapped by the quickly felting wool, and the loopy outcome resembles a luxurious, subdued bouclé.

Cross-body bags were a bit of a revelation to me. I like to joke that I could be stranded with one of my overstuffed totes and be able to survive off of the contents for a week, but when I bought my first tiny bag, I felt liberated. Edited down to the bare essentials, my entire body felt freed from the burden of schlepping around unnecessary provisions. The avian shape and one-piece construction method of the Raven Bag dawned on me at the tail end of a Seattle winter while I was immersed in Nordic culture—in particular, Odin's iconic ravens Huginn and Muninn. These anthropomorphised stand-ins for "thought" and "memory" are gorgeous reminders of a culture and history that I find endlessly inspiring.

FINISHED MEASUREMENTS
10" (25.5 cm) circumference x 12" (30.5 cm) long, not including tail, before felting

8" (20.5 cm) circumference x 11" (28 cm) long, not including tail, after felting

YARN
Berroco Lustra [50% wool / 50% Tencel; 197 yards (180 m) / 100 grams]: 2 hanks #3134 Eiffel

NEEDLES
One set of five double-pointed needles (dpn) size US 7 (4.5 mm)

One 16" (40 cm) circular (circ) needle size US 6 (4 mm)

Change needle size if necessary to obtain correct gauge.

NOTIONS
Stitch marker; two 1¾" (4.5 cm) bronze swivel clasps; 40" (101.5 cm) bronze purse chain; 9" (23 cm) non-separating zipper; 4" (10 cm) square plastic canvas; sewing needle and matching thread

GAUGE
16 sts and 22 rows = 4" (10 cm) in Stockinette stitch (St st), using larger needle, before felting

18 sts and 26 rows = 4" (10 cm) in Stockinette stitch (St st), using larger needle, after felting

TAIL

Using larger needles, CO 40 sts. Divide sts evenly among 4 needles. Join for working in the rnd, being careful not to twist sts; pm for beginning of rnd. Begin St st (knit every rnd); work even for 5 rnds.

SHAPE TAIL

RND 1: **Needle 1:** K1, k2tog, knit to end of needle; **Needle 2:** Knit to last 3 sts, ssk, k1; **Needles 3 and 4:** Repeat Needles 1 and 2—36 sts remain.

RNDS 2–10: Knit.

RNDS 11–40: Repeat Rnds 1–10—24 sts remain after Rnd 31 (6 sts each needle).

RND 41: **Needle 1:** K1, M1-r, k1, M1-l, k4; **Needle 2:** K4, M1-l, k1, M1-r, k1; **Needle 3:** K1, M1-l, knit to end of needle; **Needle 4:** Knit to last st, M1-r, k1—30 sts (8-8-7-7).

RNDS 42–48: **Needle 1:** Knit to last 3 sts, p3; **Needle 2:** P3, knit to end of needle; **Needles 3 and 4:** Knit.

RNDS 49–88: Repeat Rnds 41–48—60 sts (18-18-12-12).

BODY

SHAPE BEGINNING OF BODY

NEXT ROW (RS): Knit to end of Needle 1, turn.

ROW 1 (WS): Change to circ needle and working back and forth. Purl across Needles 1 and 4, pm, then across Needles 3 and 2.

ROW 2: K3, M1-l, knit to last 3 sts, M1-R, k3—62 sts.

ROWS 3–10: Repeat Rows 1 and 2—70 sts.

SHAPE BODY

ROW 1: Purl.

ROW 2: K3, M1-l, knit to 3 sts before marker, ssk, k1, sm, k1, k2tog, knit to last 3 sts, M1-r, k3.

Repeat Rows 1 and 2 until piece measures 8" (20.5 cm) from beginning of opening, ending with a RS row.

SHAPE END OF BODY

NOTE: *Change to dpns when necessary for number of sts on needle.*

ROW 1 (WS): Purl.

ROW 2: Knit to 3 sts before marker, ssk, k1, sm, k1, k2tog, knit to end—68 sts remain.

ROWS 3–6: Repeat Rows 1 and 2—64 sts remain.

Join for working in the rnd; pm for beginning of rnd.

RND 1: K1, ssk, knit to 3 sts before marker, k2tog, k1, sm, k1, ssk, knit to last 3 sts, k2tog, k1—60 sts remain.

RND 2: Knit.

RNDS 3–16: Repeat Rnds 1 and 2—32 sts remain.

RND 17: *K2tog; repeat from * to end—16 sts remain.

RND 18: Knit.

RNDS 19 AND 20: Repeat Rnds 17 and 18—8 sts remain. Cut yarn, leaving a 12" (30.5 cm) tail. Thread tail through sts twice, pull tight and fasten off.

FINISHING

Flatten CO edge of tail and sew closed. Felt Bag by hand in a sinkful of hot soapy water. Agitate and rub piece until sts are no longer visible. Rinse well and allow to air dry completely. Sew in zipper and attach closed end of swivel clasps at ends of Bag, ½" (1.5 cm) away from zipper. Attach opening ends of swivel clasps to chain. Cut plastic canvas to match shape of Tail and insert to hold shape. Sew across end of Tail where it meets Body.

REYKA PULLOVER

There are many reasons to visit Iceland, but for knitters, wool ranks pretty high on the list. With a robust population of sheep that haven't been crossbred since the Vikings settled the island country, Iceland is home to rich knitterly traditions that aren't relegated to museums. It's wonderful to see people of all ages wearing so much wool, even in the middle of summer. When I first traveled there, for the first time in my life, I didn't need to trot out my list of pro-wool factoids; I was among people who knew in their bones that wool is one of the very best materials on the planet.

I knit Reyka with unspun Icelandic wool, also known as *lopi*, a yarn that tends to throw unfamiliar knitters at first glance. It's sold in flat wheels that resemble 35mm film reels, and the fiber is as delicate as cotton candy. You can knit directly from the wheel with one or two plies, or you can wind a multi-ply, multi-hue yarn, adding twist or not, to suit your whims. The process revealed a lot about my knitting style. I found that I knitted with gusto, tugging the yarn violently from whatever bag or basket I'd tucked it into. This vigor did not agree with the airy *lopi*, which quickly came apart, leaving me with a truncated strand. I learned to slow down and use a gentler hand, adding a small amount of twist to the two plies as I knit. The finished fabric is soft, insulating, and, judging by the brand-new look of the well-loved *lopapeysa* I saw all over Iceland, durable.

SIZES
Small (Medium, Large, 1X-Large, 2X-Large)

FINISHED MEASUREMENTS
34½ (38½, 42½, 46½, 51)" [87.5 (98, 108, 118, 129.5) cm] bust

YARN
Ístex Plötulopi Unspun Icelandic [100% new wool; 328 yards (300 meters) / 100 grams]: 4 (5, 5, 6, 7) wheels #1033 Black Sheep Heather (MC); 1 (1, 1, 2, 2) wheel(s) #1429 Hyacinth Heather (A)

Note: If you prefer, you may substitute Ístex Létt-lopi (Lite Lopi) [100% Icelandic wool; 109 yards (99.5 meters) / 50 grams]: 6 (7, 8, 9, 9) skeins #52 Black Sheep Heather (MC); 1 (1, 2, 2, 2) skein(s) #1414 Violet Heather (A)

NEEDLES
One 16" (40 cm) long circular (circ) needle size US 8 (5 mm)

One 24" (60 cm) long circular needle size US 8 (5 mm)

One 32" (80 cm) long circular needle size US 8 (5 mm)

Change needle size if necessary to obtain correct gauge.

NOTIONS
Crochet hook size US F/5 (3.75 mm); stitch markers

GAUGE
16 sts and 20 rows = 4" (10 cm) in Stockinette stitch (St st), using 2 strands of yarn held together

NOTES
Work with 2 strands of yarn held together throughout.

STITCH PATTERNS

Two-Color Rib in the Round

(even number of sts; 2-rnd repeat)

RND 1: Using 2 strands of MC held together, *k1, p1; repeat from * to end.

RND 2: Using 2 strands of A held together, repeat Rnd 1.

Repeat Rnds 1 and 2 for *Two-Color Rib in the Round*.

Two-Color Rib Flat

(even number of sts; 2-row repeat)

ROW 1 (RS): Using 2 strands of MC held together, *k1, p1; repeat from * to end.

ROW 2: Using 2 strands of A held together, repeat Row 1.

Repeat Rows 1 and 2 for *Two-Color Rib Flat*.

BODY

Using 32" (80 cm) long circ needle and 2 strands of MC held together, CO 71 (79, 87, 95, 104) sts, pm, CO 71 (79, 87, 95, 104) sts—142 (158, 174, 190, 208) sts. Join for working in the rnd, being careful not to twist sts; pm for beginning of rnd. Begin Two-Color Rib in the Round; work even for 6 rnds. Cut A.

NEXT RND: Continuing with 2 strands of MC held together, change to St st (knit every rnd); work even until piece measures 4" (10 cm) from the beginning.

SHAPE WAIST

NEXT RND: Decrease 4 sts this rnd, then every 6 rnds 3 times, as follows: [K2, k2tog, work to 4 sts before marker, ssk, k2] twice—126 (142, 158, 174, 192) sts remain. Work even for 5 rnds.

SHAPE BUST

NEXT RND: Increase 4 sts this rnd, then every 6 rnds twice, as follows: [K2, M1-r, knit to 3 sts before marker, M1-l, k2] twice—138 (154, 170, 186, 204) sts. Work even until piece measures 14" (35.5 cm) from the beginning.

DIVIDE FOR FRONT AND BACK

NEXT RND: [Work to 5 sts before marker, BO 10 sts, removing marker] twice—59 (67, 75, 83, 92) sts remain for Front and Back.

NEXT ROW (RS): Working back and forth on Front sts only, work 4 rows in St st, beginning with a knit row. Cut yarn. Slip sts to 24" (60 cm) circ needle.

NEXT ROW (RS): With RS facing, rejoin yarn to Back sts; work 6 rows in St st, beginning with a knit row.

YOKE

With RS facing, continuing with yarn attached to Back, knit across Back sts, CO 19 (23, 33, 37, 46) sts for Left Sleeve using Backward Loop CO (see Special Techniques, page 141), knit across Front sts from second circ needle, CO 19 (23, 33, 37, 46) sts for Right Sleeve—156 (180, 216, 240, 276) sts. Join for working in the rnd, k0 (3, 1, 0, 4), pm for beginning of rnd.

NOTE: *Change to shorter circ needles when necessary for number of sts on needle.*

NEXT RND: Begin Fair Isle Chart; work Rnds 1–27, working decreases as indicated in Chart—52 (60, 72, 80, 92) sts remain.

NEXT RND: Continuing in MC, work even for 3 rnds, then work to center Front. NOTE: *Center Front should be at center of a motif, or between 2 motifs.*

HOOD

Change to working back and forth, beginning and ending at center Front.

NEXT ROW (WS): Purl, increase 1 st at center back—53 (61, 73, 81, 93) sts.

NEXT ROW (RS): Change to Two-Color Rib Flat; work even for 6 rows. Cut A.

NEXT ROW (RS): Continuing with 2 strands of MC held together, change to St st. K17 (20, 25, 28, 33), pm, k9 (10, 11, 12, 13), k2tog, k8 (9, 10, 11, 12), pm, knit to end —52 (60, 72, 80, 92) sts remain. Work even for 3 rows.

SHAPE HOOD

NEXT ROW (RS): Increase 2 sts this row, then every 4 rows 5 times, as follows: Knit to first marker, M1-r, sm, knit to next marker, sm, M1-l, knit to end—64 (72, 84, 92, 104) sts. Work even for 11 rows.

NEXT ROW (RS): Decrease 2 sts this row, then every 4 rows 3 times, as follows: Knit to 2 sts before marker, ssk, sm, knit to next marker, sm, k2tog—56 (64, 76, 84, 96) sts remain.

SHAPE TOP OF HOOD

BIND-OFF ROW (RS): BO 19 (22, 27, 30, 35) sts, removing marker, knit to next marker, remove marker, BO to end—18 (20, 22, 24, 26) sts remain. With WS facing, rejoin yarn to remaining sts. Continuing in St st, work even until top of Hood measures 4¾ (5½, 5¾, 6, 6¾)" [12 (14, 14.5, 15, 17) cm] from Bind-Off Row, ending with a WS row. BO all sts.

FAIR ISLE PATTERN

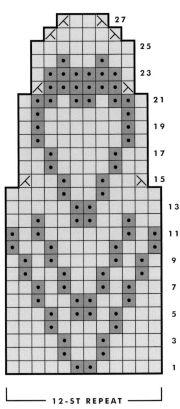

27
25
23
21
19
17
15
13
11
9
7
5
3
1

— 12-ST REPEAT —

KEY

KNIT USING MC

PURL USING A

K2TOG

SSK

FINISHING

Sew side edges of top of Hood to BO edges from Bind-Off Row.

HOOD EDGING

Using crochet hook and 1 strand of MC, and beginning at base of Hood at center Front, work 2 rnds single crochet around Hood. Fasten off.

SLEEVE EDGING

Using crochet hook and 1 strand of MC, beginning at one corner of underarm BO, work 2 rnds single crochet around Sleeve and underarm.

Block as desired.

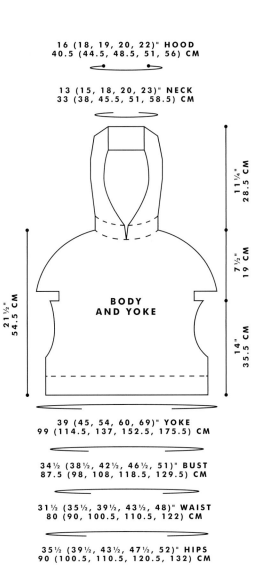

16 (18, 19, 20, 22)" HOOD
40.5 (44.5, 48.5, 51, 56) CM

13 (15, 18, 20, 23)" NECK
33 (38, 45.5, 51, 58.5) CM

11¼"
28.5 CM

7½"
19 CM

21½"
54.5 CM

BODY
AND YOKE

14"
35.5 CM

39 (45, 54, 60, 69)" YOKE
99 (114.5, 137, 152.5, 175.5) CM

34½ (38½, 42½, 46½, 51)" BUST
87.5 (98, 108, 118.5, 129.5) CM

31½ (35½, 39½, 43½, 48)" WAIST
80 (90, 100.5, 110.5, 122) CM

35½ (39½, 43½, 47½, 52)" HIPS
90 (100.5, 110.5, 120.5, 132) CM

STUDIO PULLOVER

Perhaps more than any other item in this book, saddle-shouldered Studio embodies my approach to design. It started with an irreverent slogan pulled from Kanye West's prolific and utterly entertaining Twitter feed. When he would make a mistake he would quickly correct himself, adding the hashtag #ITSAPROCESS. I loved the sentiment, and the indignant mood of the run-on, all-caps delivery. It became a mantra for me as I swatched, sketched, and ultimately rejected a whole book's worth of ideas before arriving at the keepers.

This struggle is necessary, and it reminds me of another quote I hold dear, this time from Pablo Picasso: "That inspiration comes, does not depend on me; the only thing I can do is make sure it catches me working." Studio Pullover went through many permutations, all of them serving as sketches for a moment in time—a design thought that I needed to explore. The first was a literal duplicate-stitch replica of the Kanye hashtag, but I found myself wishing for the flatter appearance of intarsia.

I painstakingly removed the lettering and grabbed a bag of vibrantly dyed curly locks, oddments from an Etsy seller comprised of the leftovers from other orders. Using the same fiber-hooking technique I chose for the Marion Collar (page 38), I covered each saddle shoulder with the locks. The effect was incredibly cool, but perhaps a bit too couture for everyday wear. I landed on a heart motif as an homage to my love for wool, something I knew most knitters would readily identify with. Before hooking the heart, I used a strand of yarn to roughly outline where I wanted the motif. This spare, geometric heart with two dangling tails at the bottom formed a third, wholly unexpected incarnation, one that I plan to replicate in another sweater, perhaps with lightweight chain.

Studio ended up taking many more hours than it should have, but it felt like tending a bonsai. Each variation bent my will in a new way, forcing a thorough exploration of my goals and my perception of the audience. As ever, it's a process....

SIZES
To fit bust sizes 32 (34, 36, 38, 40, 42, 44, 48, 52)" [81.5 (86.5, 91.5, 96.5, 101.5, 106.5, 112, 122, 132) cm]

FINISHED MEASUREMENTS
36¾ (38½, 40, 43¼, 44¾, 46½, 48, 51¼, 56)" [93.5 (98, 101.5, 110, 113.5, 118, 122, 130, 142) cm] bust

YARN
Manos del Uruguay Rittenhouse 5-Ply [100% merino wool; 240 yards (219.5 meters) / 100 grams]: 4 (4, 5, 5, 5, 5, 6, 6, 7) hanks #544 Briar (MC)

Manos del Uruguay Maxima [100% merino wool; 219 (200 meters) / 100 grams]: small amount of #M2060 Highlighter (A)

4 ounces (114.5 grams) Hippie Chix Fiber Art loose curly locks in mixed colors

NEEDLES
One set of five doubled-pointed needles (dpn) size US 6 (4 mm)

One set of five doubled-pointed needles size US 7 (4.5 mm)

One 32" (80 cm) long circular (circ) needle size US 6 (4 mm)

One 32" (80 cm) long circular needle size US 7 (4.5 mm)

Change needle size if necessary to obtain correct gauge.

NOTIONS
Crochet hook size US F/5 (3.75 mm); stitch markers; waste yarn or stitch holder; safety pins; tapestry needle (optional)

GAUGE
20 sts and 24 rows = 4" (10 cm) in Stockinette stitch (St st), using larger needles

STITCH PATTERNS

Body Rib
(multiple of 4 sts; 1-rnd repeat)
ALL RNDS: [P1, *k2, p2; repeat from * to 3 sts before marker, k2, p1] twice.

Sleeve Rib
(multiple of 4 sts; 1-rnd repeat)
ALL RNDS: *K2, p2; repeat from * to end.

Crab Stitch Edging
ROW 1 (SINGLE CROCHET):
Work from right to left for right-handers, or from left to right for left-handers. Make a slipknot and place on hook. *Insert hook into next st (for working horizontal edge) or between two rows (for working vertical edge). Yo hook, pull through to RS–2 loops on hook. Yo hook, draw through both loops–1 loop on hook. Repeat from * to end. NOTE: *It may be necessary to skip a row every so often when working along a vertical edge, in order to prevent puckering.*

ROW 2 (REVERSE SINGLE CROCHET): Work from left to right for right-handers, or from right to left for left-handers. *Insert hook into previous single crochet, yo hook, pull through to RS–2 loops on hook. Yo hook, draw through both loops–1 loop on hook. Repeat from * to end. Fasten off.

BODY

Using smaller circ needle and MC, CO 92 (96, 100, 108, 112, 116, 120, 128, 140) sts, pm, CO 92 (96, 100, 108, 112, 116, 120, 128, 140) sts—184 (192, 200, 216, 224, 232, 240, 256, 280) sts. Join for working in the rnd, being careful not to twist sts; pm for beginning of rnd. Begin Body Rib; work even until piece measures 1½" (4 cm) from the beginning.

NEXT RND: Change to larger circ needle. [P1, knit to 1 st before marker, p1] twice. Work even until piece measures 14½ (14½, 15, 15, 15½, 15½, 16, 16, 16½)" [37 (37, 38, 38, 39.5, 39.5, 40.5, 40.5, 42) cm] from the beginning, ending last rnd 5 (5, 5, 6, 5, 6, 6, 7, 9) sts before beginning-of-rnd marker.

DIVIDE FOR FRONT AND BACK

NEXT RND: BO 10 (10, 10, 12, 10, 12, 12, 14, 18) sts, removing marker, knit to 5 (5, 5, 6, 5, 6, 6, 7, 9) sts before next marker, place last 82 (86, 90, 96, 102, 104, 108, 114, 122) sts on waste yarn or st holder for Front, BO 10 (10, 10, 12, 10, 12, 12, 14, 18) sts, removing marker, knit to end—82 (86, 90, 96, 102, 104, 108, 114, 122) sts remain for Back.

BACK

Working on Back sts only, purl 1 row.

SHAPE ARMHOLES

NEXT ROW (RS): Decrease 1 st each side this row, then every other row 12 (13, 14, 15, 16, 17, 18, 20, 22) times, as follows: K1, k2tog, knit to last 3 sts, ssk, k1—56 (58, 60, 64, 68, 68, 70, 72, 76) sts remain. Purl 1 row.

SHAPE SHOULDERS

NEXT ROW (RS): BO 5 (6, 7, 7, 7, 7, 7, 8, 9) sts at beginning of next 2 rows. BO remaining 46 (46, 46, 50, 54, 54, 56, 56, 58) sts.

FRONT

With RS facing, rejoin yarn to sts on waste yarn for Front. Complete as for Back.

SLEEVES

Using smaller dpns and MC, CO 44 (44, 48, 48, 48, 52, 52, 52, 52) sts. Join for working in the rnd, being careful not to twist sts; pm for beginning of rnd. Begin Sleeve Rib; work even until piece measures 1½" (4 cm) from the beginning.

NEXT RND: Change to larger dpns and St st. Work even for 1 rnd.

SHAPE SLEEVE

NEXT RND: Increase 2 sts this rnd, every 8 (8, 8, 6, 6, 6, 6, 4, 4) rnds 2 (6, 5, 3, 6, 5, 8, 4, 16) times, then every 10 (10, 10, 8, 8, 8, 8, 6, 6) rnds 6 (3, 4, 8, 6, 7, 5, 12, 4) times, as follows: K2, M1-l, knit to last 2 sts, M1-r, k2 —62 (64, 68, 72, 74, 78, 80, 86, 94) sts. Work even until piece measures 16 (16½, 16¾, 17, 17½, 17¾, 18¼, 18¼, 18¼)" [40.5 (42, 42.5, 43, 44.5, 45, 46.5, 46.5, 46.5) cm] from the beginning, ending last rnd 5 (5, 5, 6, 5, 6, 6, 7, 9) sts before marker.

SHAPE CAP

NEXT RND: BO 10 (10, 10, 12, 10, 12, 12, 14, 18) sts, removing marker, knit to end—52 (54, 58, 60, 64, 66, 68, 72, 76) sts remain. Purl 1 row.

NEXT ROW (RS): BO 3 sts at beginning of next 2 rows, then decrease 1 st each side every other row 11 (11, 13, 14, 14, 15, 17, 17, 18) times, then every 4 rows 1 (2, 1, 1, 2, 2, 1, 2, 3) time(s), as follows: K1, k2tog, work to last 3 sts, ssk, k1. BO 4 sts at beginning of next 2 rows—14 (14, 16, 16, 18, 18, 18, 20, 20) sts remain.

SHAPE SADDLE

NEXT ROW: Work even until Saddle measures 3½ (3½, 3½, 3½, 4, 4, 4, 4, 4)" [9 (9, 9, 9, 10, 10, 10, 10, 10) cm] from last BO row, ending with a WS row. BO all sts.

FINISHING

Place markers approximately 1¼ (1¼, 1¼, 1½, 1½, 1½, 1¾, 1¾, 1¾)" [3 (3, 3, 4, 4, 4, 4.5, 4.5, 4.5) cm] to either side of center of BO edge of Back and Front. Pin straight side edge of one Saddle to BO edge of Front, between marker and end of BO edge. Pin opposite edge of same Saddle to BO edge of Back. Sew in Sleeve. Repeat for second Sleeve.

NECKBAND

Using crochet hook and A and beginning at left Back Saddle seam, work Crab Stitch Edging around neck edge.

Block as desired.

CURLY LOCKS HEART

Trace the outline of a heart on the Front using a loose running st, tapestry needle, and waste yarn (optional). With RS facing, insert crochet hook into knitted fabric inside heart outline (making sure to avoid thread) and pull one end of lock through to RS, then move ½" (1.5 cm) in any direction (staying within heart outline) and pull opposite end of lock through to RS. Continue in this manner, pulling locks through randomly until entire heart is filled with locks. Remove heart outline.

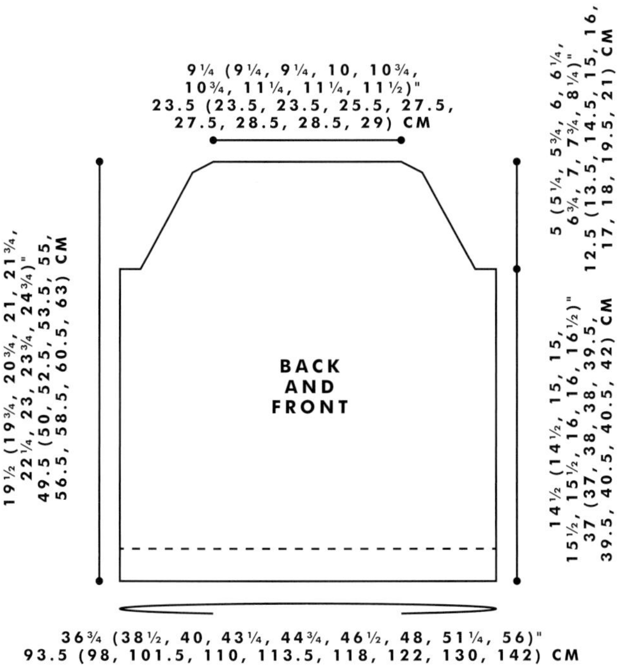
9¼ (9¼, 9¼, 10, 10¾, 10¾, 11¼, 11¼, 11½)"
23.5 (23.5, 23.5, 25.5, 27.5, 27.5, 28.5, 28.5, 29) CM
19½ (19¾, 20¾, 21, 21¾, 22¼, 23, 23¾, 24¾)"
49.5 (50, 52.5, 53.5, 55, 56.5, 58.5, 60.5, 63) CM
BACK AND FRONT
5 (5¼, 5¾, 6, 6¼, 6¾, 7, 7¾, 8¼)"
12.5 (13.5, 14.5, 15, 16, 17, 18, 19.5, 21) CM
14½ (14½, 15, 15, 15½, 15½, 16, 16, 16½)"
37 (37, 38, 38, 39.5, 39.5, 40.5, 40.5, 42) CM
36¾ (38½, 40, 43¼, 44¾, 46½, 48, 51¼, 56)"
93.5 (98, 101.5, 110, 113.5, 118, 122, 130, 142) CM

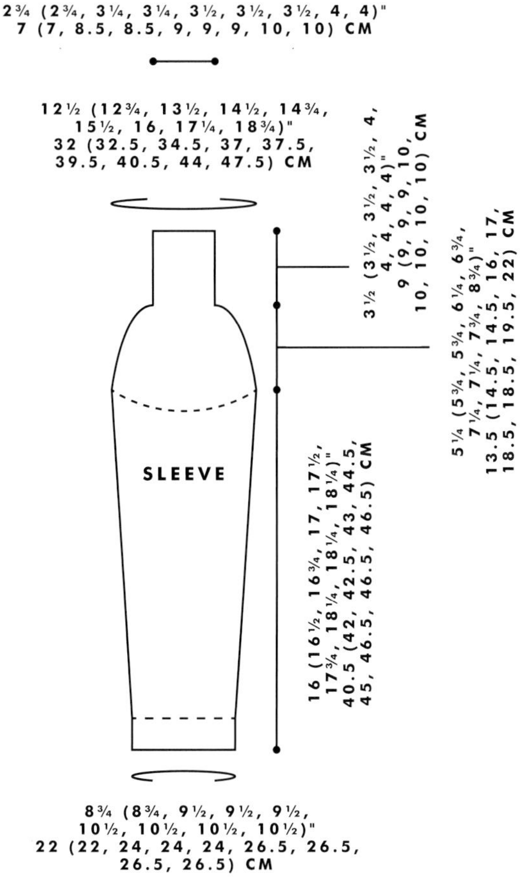
2¾ (2¾, 3¼, 3¼, 3½, 3½, 3½, 4, 4)"
7 (7, 8.5, 8.5, 9, 9, 9, 10, 10) CM
12½ (12¾, 13½, 14½, 14¾, 15½, 16, 17¼, 18¾)"
32 (32.5, 34.5, 37, 37.5, 39.5, 40.5, 44, 47.5) CM
3½ (3½, 3½, 3½, 4, 4, 4, 4, 4)"
9 (9, 9, 9, 10, 10, 10, 10, 10) CM
5¼ (5¾, 5¾, 6¼, 6¾, 7¼, 7¼, 7¾, 8¾)"
13.5 (14.5, 14.5, 16, 17, 18.5, 18.5, 19.5, 22) CM
SLEEVE
16 (16½, 16¾, 17, 17½, 17¾, 18¼, 18¼, 18¼)"
40.5 (42, 42.5, 43, 44.5, 45, 46.5, 46.5, 46.5) CM
8¾ (8¾, 9½, 9½, 9½, 10½, 10½, 10½, 10½)"
22 (22, 24, 24, 24, 26.5, 26.5, 26.5, 26.5) CM

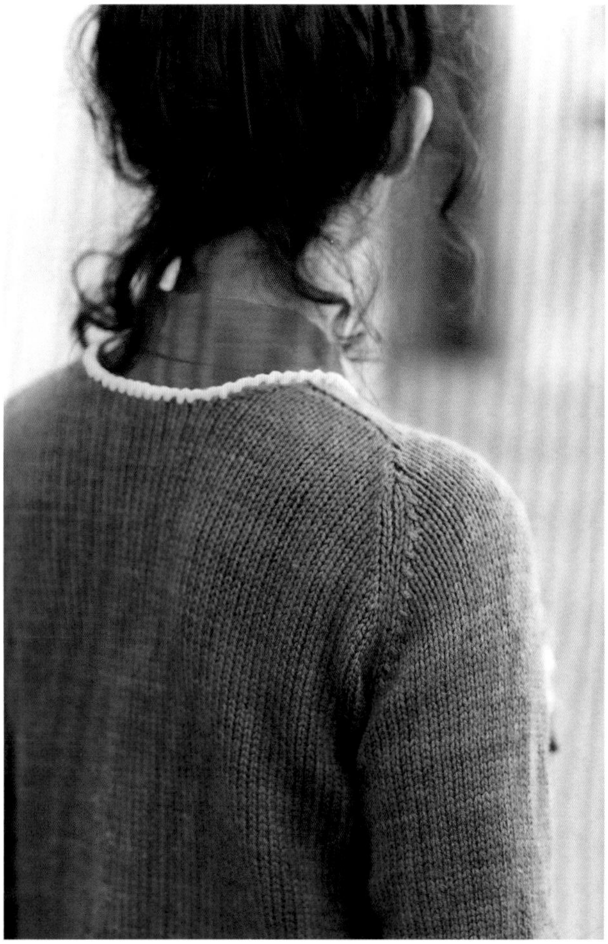

FINDING MYSELF IN ICELAND

AS A MILITARY KID, I GREW UP ALL OVER THE WORLD. MY PARENTS INSTILLED IN
MY SIBLINGS AND ME AN AVID CURIOSITY ABOUT OTHER CULTURES, ALWAYS
OPTING TO PLUNGE US INTO THE CENTER OF WHATEVER COUNTRY WE WERE
LIVING IN RATHER THAN HAVING US LIVE APART ON MILITARY BASES. THE
WANDERLUST THAT RESULTED IS NOW PART OF WHO I AM, FOR BETTER OR
WORSE. AT TIMES THE JUMBLE OF MEMORIES AND EXPERIENCES FROM ALL
OF THE MOVING AROUND I HAVE DONE LEAVES ME WITH A ROOTLESS AND
CHAOTIC FEELING, BUT MORE OFTEN THAN NOT, IT ALSO CREATES THE PERFECT
ENVIRONMENT FOR FOMENTING IDEAS, ESPECIALLY ABOUT DESIGN AND STYLE.
I'VE NEVER FELT AS INSPIRED OR AS AT HOME AS WHEN I VISIT ICELAND.

I confess my interest in Iceland began as a teenager
in the early '90s with a singer called Björk. Most
notorious for the peculiar swan dress she wore to
perform at the Oscars and her quirky behavior
in interviews, she was the butt of a lot of jokes,
and sadly, so was Iceland. Nevertheless, with my
voracious teenage appetite for new and different, I
felt I'd found a soulmate in this esoteric, eccentric
celebrity. When I finally got the chance to visit her
home country as an adult, I found that she was
not an anomaly, but rather, a hyper-distillation of
Iceland itself.

I never could have guessed that knitting would be
my way into Iceland, but it was. My first visit was
organized by my dear friend Ragnheiður Eiríksdóttir.
It was a teaching trip with another kindred spirit,
Stephen West. Before touring the countryside with
a group of eager knitters, Stephen, Ragga, and
I planned a photo shoot. This shoot involved an
American colleague and friend, photographer Jared
Flood (who also shot this book). We spent one long
weekend in the north, shooting gorgeous knits on
gorgeous models and trying to get over the fact that
we were in Iceland.

Simply being in Iceland is enough to move your
soul. Anyone with even a tenuous connection to
nature will find themselves enthralled by the vast
expanses that seem to change every minute, each
one more beautiful than the last. Every Icelander
seems to be intrinsically connected to their
landscape. This reverence is something I identified
with immediately. In a tumultuous life, nature
has always been a constant. Wherever I am and
whatever I'm feeling, retreating to the woods or the
oceanside is a healing ritual than never disappoints,
and Icelanders seem to know this in their bones.
They never look at me cross-eyed when I talk about
trees as though they're my friends.

Another cultural imperative that I find completely
endearing is the need to create. Björk articulates
this in many interviews, and many of her countryfolk
and contemporaries echo the sentiment. There
are theories that the long dark winter necessitates
artistic pursuits. Others attribute the interest in
writing, storytelling, singing, and music-making to
the island's Viking founders. Whatever the reason,
it is much more than a token interest. Nearly every
Icelandic person I've met has at least two hobbies
and usually a job they are passionately interested

in. They manage to balance worldliness and fierce national pride in a way that creates a singular blend of idiosyncratic intelligence.

I haven't even gotten to the best part! Icelanders wear wool like no one else on the planet. Icelandic sheep produce incredibly unique fiber and have never been crossbred since their arrival in the ninth century. The first time I felt Lopi wool, I found it rather coarse. It had a strange crunch that reminded me of steel wool. It wasn't until I learned the purpose of blending *tog*, the soft, downy undercoat, and *thel*, the longer water-resistant tendrils of the outer fleece, that I understood the unique, nearly weatherproof properties of Icelandic wool. The ubiquity of this type of wool is fascinating and a wonderful reminder of the fact that restraint can often lead to inspired design. Flat wheels of the unspun *plötulopi*, tiny skeins of laceweight *einband,* and big ropey hanks of the bulky version are available nearly everywhere in Iceland in the exact same gorgeous color palette.

The raw materials serve as a common denominator, but the finished objects I've seen made with the Icelandic wool could not be more distinctive or more covetable. From a pillow from product designer Marý emblazoned with Icelandic virtues to the full-body adult-sized seal suit from the Vík Prjónsdóttir, from Ragga's modern top-down update of the traditional *lopapeysa* sweater to the leopard-print jacquard coat I purchased from Icelandic label Farmers Market, each item has a soul of its own while feeling firmly Icelandic.

I've landed in Seattle for now, a sister city to my beloved Reykjavik. It's easy to draw comparisons between the two cities, and the pastiche of cultures in Seattle is never dilute—like Icelanders, Seattleites have a fierce pride for their roots, whether those roots are in Vietnam, Japan, Scandinavia, or First Nations. There is also a reverence for creating.

Whether it is code or comic books, nearly everyone I meet has a creative pilot light that guides them through the long gray winters. Knitting is, of course, mine, and Iceland has reaffirmed that. My thoughts on construction and scale expand with every visit and find their way into my designs and wardrobe. The Gezell Coat (page 98 and below) is a harbinger of this direction—classic and moody in all black, but knit in an unusual way as two halves, with a generous amount of slouchy ease. This is the kind of coat I see all over Reykjavik, tossed on and off impossibly tall bodies as they flit from cafe to gallery to grocery store. It's a statement cardigan, made even more dramatic with the addition of a bit of fur, another Icelandic hallmark.

I'm attempting to learn Icelandic, and it's fun for many reasons, most of all because speaking it seems to require passion, something Icelanders have a surplus of (though in true Nordic fashion, it lives under a layer of easily broken ice at times). I'll leave you with my favorite phrase, something to be shouted with gusto: *gaman að sjá þig!* It means "Fun to see you," and it truly is.

LOOKING FOR A COME-UP (AKA THRIFTING)

IN 2012, PACIFIC NORTHWEST RAPPER MACKLEMORE TOOK THE ENTIRE WORLD BY STORM WITH HIS SONG "THRIFT SHOP," VALIDATING AN ACTIVITY THAT USED TO MAKE ME BURN WITH SHAME. "I'M GONNA POP SOME TAGS, ONLY GOT TWENTY DOLLARS IN MY POCKET, I-I-I'M HUNTING, LOOKING FOR A COME-UP..." IT DOESN'T SURPRISE ME AT ALL THAT THIS THUMPING, JOYOUS ODE TO THRIFTING CAME FROM THE PRACTICAL, ECO-CONSCIOUS CITY OF SEATTLE, BECAUSE I'VE HAD SOME OF THE BEST THRIFT SCORES OF MY LIFE HERE.

I've been thrifting my entire life. What started as a necessity turned into one of my most enjoyable obsessions. As a young, label-conscious preteen I hated that my clothes were secondhand, but after years of honing my hunting skills, I know the unique thrill of scoring a pristine designer item for less than a pizza, and I'm HOOKED. Besides that, it's become a low-risk way to experiment with new-to-me silhouettes, colors, and cuts.

It's important to make a distinction between the vintage shopping normally recommended in style manuals and magazines and what Macklemore is rapping about. I am much more familiar with the latter, which is decidedly déclassé. I'm a frugal omnivore, so I do frequent the calm, clean consignment boutiques where you can hardly tell that clothing has been worn before. The prices are higher there and finding serviceable garments is almost a given, but the rush of finding an amazing piece on-the-cheap is lacking.

Shopping in thrift stores isn't just wonderful for your bank account. It's a style boot camp, and it can be just as exhausting as the real deal. If you're looking to refresh your look or completely reinvent yourself, combing through endless racks will force you to zero in on what you love and what works on you. For the hand-knitter, it's also a fantastic way to test-drive a type of sweater before committing to making your own. Not sure if saddle shoulders will flatter your figure? Find one at the thrift store and wear it for a weekend to see how it feels.

Besides new underpinnings for your latest handknits, you are sure to see plenty of what I call wool tragedies. Every thrift store I've ever visited has them. Sad, shrunken, felted Arans and firmly felted Fair Isles. Sigh. Some poor, uninitiated soul tossed a gorgeous sweater into the wash and ruined a perfectly lovely 100% wool garment. Tragic. But, as a wool lover you know full well that there is plenty of upcycling potential here. Those sweaters deserve to be redeemed, and they can be cut and turned into all sorts of useful objects. A bit of embroidery or some knit-on ribbing and you can have a laptop cozy or a pair of legwarmers in no time.

You can go in with a list, but it's better to be open-minded about what you might find. If you're diligent, you'll begin to know that you always find designer-label jeans at the one Goodwill on the outskirts of town, or that the upcycling boutique near the university sells refashioned Japanese dresses that everyone will ask you about. Cultivate your own disparate department store. You are a knitter, and one-of-a-kind knits deserve an equally eclectic backdrop.

Since you won't have the "benefit" of seeing a collection presented as stiff ensembles on faceless mannequins, you will have to fire up your imagination. This is where a bit of preparation and thought can save you hours. When I go thrift shopping, I know going in what kinds of items I need, what I absolutely need NO more of, and what sort of character I'm channeling that season. I flip through the racks with fervor in the beginning, grabbing colors, prints, and silhouettes I find intriguing. Stay open; this is where you can and should play with things you're just not sure about.

Drag your haul to a mirror and hold each piece up. They need to pass this basic screening before you actually try on, and if they don't, move along. Personally, I try to leave behind any items that need special care or additional clothing to work. I know myself, and it will never get done. The most effort I'm willing to exert is a thorough handwashing or a trip to the dry cleaner's, and maybe a button upgrade. The best pieces arrive and feel instantly at home in your wardrobe. You forget where you found them because you feel like you've owned them forever.

Regarding washing! It's true—shopping in large, unfancy thrift shops is not for the faint of heart. Pace yourself, stay hydrated, and bring some antibacterial wipes for your hands. When you get your new items home, treat them to a bath, or several! I love to use Soak, which is meant for knitwear (my favorite scent is Celebration). If an item has an unfortunate lingering mustiness, attack it with a baking soda solution, then hang the garment in the sun for a while (monitor it to make sure the colors aren't fading). These three tricks will almost always render a garment wholly fresh. Consider it a fashion baptism.

THE CANON

RECOMMENDED READING

I AM AS PASSIONATE ABOUT BOOKS AS I AM ABOUT YARN. BOOKS BOAST A QUIET, ABSORBING QUALITY AND HOLD THE TANTALIZING PROSPECT OF SELF-IMPROVEMENT. AT THE OUTSET, THEY'RE SHINY, COLORFUL NEW FRIENDS, EXTENSIONS OF OUR TASTES AND OBSESSIONS. AS THE YEARS PASS, THEY AGE ALONGSIDE US, ACCUMULATING MEMORIES AND SERVING AS RELIABLE PORTALS TO EARLIER ITERATIONS OF OURSELVES.

I TRY TO MAKE REGULAR EDITS TO MY LIBRARY TO MAKE SURE THERE IS NOTHING THERE WITHOUT A PURPOSE. HERE ARE SOME RECENT FAVORITES AND STALWART TOMES.

ALL-AROUND GEMS

KNITTER'S ALMANAC
BY ELIZABETH ZIMMERMANN

Back in my LYS days, I sold a copy of this nearly every shift I worked. For the price of two lattes, customers were getting solid gold knitting information, patterns, personal pep talks, and a genuinely funny memoir. This is my deserted island knitting book.

THE KNITTER'S BOOK OF YARN
BY CLARA PARKES

A crash course in fibers from the Julia Child of yarn, my friend Clara Parkes. Knowing your yarn is half the battle, and Clara will tell you how to make your yarn reveal itself.

INSPIRATION

SCHIAPARELLI & PRADA: IMPOSSIBLE CONVERSATIONS
BY ANDREW BOLTON

When I was in graduate school, an easy way to fake highbrow critique was to say that two things were "in conversation." This book, a catalogue from the eponymous museum exhibit, finally gave that phrase meaning for me. What a gorgeous and humbling gift to listen in on this imagined conversation, and to be reminded that none of us is working in a vacuum.

ALEXANDER MCQUEEN: SAVAGE BEAUTY
BY ANDREW BOLTON

So beautiful, it hurts. Do you have a taste for the macabre? Does the natural world level you with you its brutal splendor? Then you'll find a kindred spirit in McQueen.

THE ONE HUNDRED
BY NINA GARCIA

A crash course in fashion history, with whimsical illustrations by Ruben Toledo, this book is actually a very compelling checklist for a practical, high-functioning wardrobe. Trust this editrix!

THE FASHION FILE
BY JANIE BRYANT

A must for any *Mad Men* fan. Head costumer Janie Bryant revels in femininity and old Hollywood glamour, which is exactly why the women on *Mad Men* always look so incredible. For bonus points, I recommend reading Mad Style posts on the Tom and Lorenzo blog. Screen captures and costume factoids galore!

SECOND-TIME COOL
BY ANNA-STINA LINDEN IVARSSON, KATARINA BRIEDITIS, AND KATARINA EVANS

An exceedingly inspiring Scandinavian take on upcycling and embellishment.

LOOP-D-LOOP SERIES
BY TEVA DURHAM

No one writes or thinks about knitting the way Teva does in this three-book series, and I absolutely love it. Her references are obscure and her perspective askew; the resulting garments are endlessly unique.

I LOVE YOUR STYLE
BY AMANDA BROOKS

Style categories like minimal, high fashion, and street are masterfully explained and illustrated, but Brooks is never didactic. Rather, she puts fashion's most willful individuals under a microscope, distilling the efficacy of their looks into easily understood key points.

THE GENTLE ART OF DOMESTICITY
BY JANE BROCKET

When I was a student at UMass/Amherst, I spent a lot of time on one of the very top floors of the record-breakingly tall library, on the floor where all of the home economics texts were shelved. The home economics department was shut down long before I arrived at UMass, but I spent many snowy evenings poring over the cookbooks, sewing manuals, and women's magazines on this floor. Jane's gorgeous collection of essays and photos gives me the same feeling of calm and awe that I felt in those stacks.

ICELANDIC KNITTING: USING ROSE PATTERNS
BY HÉLÈNE MAGNÚSSON

This ode to a very specific style of intarsia found on a very specific item (shoe inserts) is actually one of the most refreshing knitting books I've ever come across, mostly because of the photography, which is playful, bold, and full of natural beauty, just like Iceland.

POP KNITTING: BOLD MOTIFS USING COLOR & STITCH
BY BRITT-MARIE CHRISTOFFERSSON

A slightly bonkers stitch dictionary unlike any other, full of surface design and strange textural effects. The mind reels, in a very good way.

KNIT A FANTASY STORY
BY JAN MESSENT

All self-respecting nerds should own this book. I do, and when I retire from professional knitting I will knit myself a Middle Earth.

KNITTING IN THE NORDIC TRADITION
BY VIBEKE LIND

I don't even have to open this book to feel inspired by it. The cover is just that good. There are plenty of treasures inside though, practical time-tested blueprints, history and geography lessons, and incredible photos.

TECHNIQUE

KNITTER'S HANDBOOK
BY MONTSE STANLEY

This hefty volume is full of thorough explanations and hard-to-find techniques, all written in a friendly but authoritative tone. It reminds me of Irma Rombauer's *Joy of Cooking*, simultaneously encyclopedic and chatty. Even if you only have five minutes to flip through, you will stumble upon something that will enrich your knitting.

VOGUE KNITTING: THE ULTIMATE KNITTING BOOK (+ QUICK REFERENCE VERSION)

These straightforward guides form the basis of my knitting knowledge. I used the tables in the back of this book to try to cobble together my very first sweater design, a black cardigan inspired by Kurt Cobain. I never finished it, but I still consult the books almost daily.

THE STITCH 'N BITCH SERIES
BY DEBBIE STOLLER

It makes total sense that Debbie's books are empowering, informative, and fun—she edits *Bust*, one of the most fun feminist magazines around. I will fully admit to geeking out big time when I finally met her. I couldn't help it—she is the coolest.

THE PRINCIPLES OF KNITTING
BY JUNE HEMMONS HIATT

I daydream about working my way through this book the way Julie Powell famously sauteed her way through *Mastering the Art of French Cooking*. I lived through the infamous dark ages where this book was out of print and would regularly sell for hundreds of dollars on eBay. I would hold library copies hostage for weeks at a time, and I never even came close to consuming all that glorious and occasionally brazen information. I am by no means a perfect or dogmatic knitter, but you have to know the rules before you break them, right?

THE KNITTER'S BOOK OF FINISHING TECHNIQUES
BY NANCIE WISEMAN

Give yourself the time to do a wonderful job finishing the sweater that took hours and hours to knit. Your knitting deserves that! I promise, it can be fun. Wine helps.

ANY BOOK BY MAGGIE RIGHETTI

Maggie Righetti is hilarious and informative. How can you not love a knitter who wrote a whole chapter called "Buttonholes Are Bastards"? She also taught me two of the most invaluable tips of my knitting career: "Stop often and admire your work," and "It's not a mistake if you know how you made it." It's amazing how many mistakes I catch when I'm "admiring."

KNIT YOUR OWN LOPAPEYSA
BY RAGNHEIÐUR EIRÍKSDÓTTIR

A bit of a cheat, this is actually a DVD made by an Icelandic friend, but I watch it whenever I am "homesick" for Iceland, a place where I felt deeply understood and inspired as a knitter and wool obsessive.

SOURCES

FOR SUPPLIES

FOLLOWING IS A LIST OF THE COMPANIES THAT SUPPLIED THE YARN AND BUTTONS FOR THE PROJECTS FEATURED IN THIS BOOK. IF YOU CAN'T FIND THEM AT YOUR FAVORITE LYS, CONTACT THESE COMPANIES FOR HELP.

BERROCO YARNS INC.
WWW.BERROCO.COM
Raven Bag (BERROCO LUSTRA)

CASCADE
WWW.CASCADEYARNS.COM
Coterie Cardigan (CASCADE ECOLOGICAL WOOL)

FAIRMOUNT FIBERS
WWW.FAIRMOUNTFIBERS.COM
Framboise Cardigan + Scarf (MANOS DEL URUGUAY SILK BLEND), *Studio Pullover* (MANOS DEL URUGUAY RITTENHOUSE 5-PLY + MANOS DEL URUGUAY MAXIMA)

HIPPIE CHIX FIBER ART
HIPPIECHIXFIBER.ETSY.COM
Marion Collar (HIPPIE CHIX FIBER ART LOOSE CURLY LOCKS), *Studio Pullover* (HIPPIE CHIX FIBER ART LOOSE CURLY LOCKS)

JADE SAPPHIRE EXOTIC FIBRES
WWW.JADESAPPHIRE.COM
Levitt Hat (JADE SAPPHIRE EXOTIC FIBRES HANDSPUN CASHMERE)

JHB BUTTONS
WWW.BUTTONS.COM
Coterie Cardigan (NICKY EPSTEIN DEAD KING #92734)

KELBOURNE WOOLENS
WWW.KELBOURNEWOOLENS.COM
L'Arbre Hat + Mitts (THE FIBRE COMPANY ROAD TO CHINA WORSTED), *Tisane Tank* (THE FIBRE COMPANY SAVANNAH DK), *Lana Cowl* (THE FIBRE COMPANY ORGANIK)

KFI
WWW.KNITTINGFEVER.COM
Breve Cowl (NORO SILK GARDEN), *Tasse Mug / Pint Cozy* (NORO KUREYON)

O-WOOL
WWW.O-WOOL.COM
Kosi Cowl (O-WOOL BALANCE BULKY)

MADELINETOSH
WWW.MADELINETOSH.COM
Loro Vest (MADELINETOSH TOSH MERINO)

NEIGHBORHOOD FIBER CO.
WWW.NEIGHBORHOODFIBERCO.COM
Garance Camisole (NEIGHBORHOOD FIBER CO. PENTHOUSE SILK FINGERING)

ONE WORLD BUTTON SUPPLY CO.
WWW.ONEWORLDBUTTONS.COM
Framboise Cardigan

PEACE FLEECE
WWW.PEACEFLEECE.COM
Jordaan Cape (PEACE FLEECE WORSTED WEIGHT)

SIRRI
WWW.SIRRI.FO
WWW.FAROEKNITTING.COM
Jordaan Cape (SIRRI SIRRITÓGV 2-PLY COLOUR)

SCHOOLHOUSE PRESS
WWW.SCHOOLHOUSEPRESS.COM
Reyka Pullover (ÍSTEX PLÖTULOPI UNSPUN ICELANDIC)

SKACEL COLLECTION INC.
WWW.SKACELKNITTING.COM
Karin Fascinator (SCHULANA KID-PAILLETTES), *Norah Hat* (HIKOO KENZIE), *Borgarnes Pillow* (HIKOO TEE-CAKES), *Heima Slippers* (SCHOPPEL-WOLLE RELIKT), *Marion Collar* (SCHULANA LAMBSWOOL + SCHULANA ANGORA FASHION PRINT), *Meta Tee* (HIKOO TEE-CAKES) *Gezell Coat* (SCHULANA ROYALPACA), *Rainier Cowl* (HIKOO SIMPLIWORSTED + HIKOO CARIBOU)

WESTMINSTER FIBERS
WWW.WESTMINSTERFIBERS.COM
Breve Cowl (ROWAN DENIM)

THE YARN SISTERS INC.
WWW.THEYARNSISTERS.COM
Isla Cardigan (ZEALANA RIMU DK), *Karin Fascinator* (ZEALANA PERFORMA KAURI WORSTED WEIGHT)

ABBREVIATIONS

BO   BIND OFF

CIRC   CIRCULAR

CN   CABLE NEEDLE

CO   CAST ON

DPN   DOUBLE-POINTED NEEDLE(S)

K1-F/B   KNIT INTO THE FRONT LOOP AND BACK LOOP OF THE SAME STITCH TO INCREASE 1 STITCH.

K1-TBL   KNIT 1 STITCH THROUGH THE BACK LOOP.

K2TOG   KNIT 2 STITCHES TOGETHER.

K3TOG   KNIT 3 STITCHES TOGETHER.

K   KNIT

M1 OR M1-L (MAKE 1-LEFT SLANTING) WITH THE TIP OF THE LEFT-HAND NEEDLE INSERTED FROM FRONT TO BACK, LIFT THE STRAND BETWEEN THE 2 NEEDLES ONTO THE LEFT-HAND NEEDLE; KNIT THE STRAND THROUGH THE BACK LOOP TO INCREASE 1 STITCH.

M1-R (MAKE 1-RIGHT SLANTING) WITH THE TIP OF THE LEFT-HAND NEEDLE INSERTED FROM BACK TO FRONT, LIFT THE STRAND BETWEEN THE 2 NEEDLES ONTO THE LEFT-HAND NEEDLE; KNIT THE STRAND THROUGH THE FRONT LOOP TO INCREASE 1 STITCH.

MB   MAKE BOBBLE (AS INSTRUCTED).

P2TOG   PURL 2 STITCHES TOGETHER.

PM   PLACE MARKER

P   PURL

PSSO (PASS SLIPPED STITCH OVER) PASS THE SLIPPED STITCH ON THE RIGHT-HAND NEEDLE OVER THE STITCH(ES) INDICATED IN THE INSTRUCTIONS, AS IN BINDING OFF.

REV   REVERSE

RND(S)   ROUND(S)

RS   RIGHT SIDE

S2KP2   SLIP THE NEXT 2 STITCHES TOGETHER TO THE RIGHT-HAND NEEDLE AS IF TO KNIT 2 TOGETHER, K1, PASS THE 2 SLIPPED STITCHES OVER.

SM   SLIP MARKER

SSK (SLIP, SLIP, KNIT)   SLIP THE NEXT 2 STITCHES TO THE RIGHT-HAND NEEDLE ONE AT A TIME AS IF TO KNIT; RETURN THEM TO THE LEFT-HAND NEEDLE ONE AT A TIME IN THEIR NEW ORIENTATION; KNIT THEM TOGETHER THROUGH THE BACK LOOPS.

ST(S)   STITCH(ES)

TBL   THROUGH THE BACK LOOP

TOG   TOGETHER

WS   WRONG SIDE

WRP-T   WRAP AND TURN (SEE SPECIAL TECHNIQUES: SHORT ROW SHAPING)

WYIB   WITH YARN IN BACK

WYIF   WITH YARN IN FRONT

YO   YARNOVER (SEE SPECIAL TECHNIQUES)

SPECIAL TECHNIQUES

BACKWARD LOOP CO

Make a loop (using a slip knot) with the working yarn and place it on the right-hand needle (first st CO), *wind yarn around thumb clockwise, insert right-hand needle into the front of the loop on thumb, remove thumb and tighten st on needle; repeat from * for remaining sts to be CO, or for casting on at the end of a row in progress.

CABLE CO

Make a loop (using a slip knot) with the working yarn and place it on the left-hand needle (first st CO), knit into slip knot, draw up a loop but do not drop st from left-hand needle; place new loop on left-hand needle; *insert the tip of the right-hand needle into the space between the last 2 sts on the left-hand needle and draw up a loop; place the loop on the left-hand needle. Repeat from * for remaining sts to be CO, or for casting on at the end of a row in progress.

CAT BORDHI'S MOEBIUS CO

Make a slipknot, place it on circular needle, and slide it to center of cable of needle. Holding slipknot in place with left hand, bring left-hand end of needle around so that tip is pointing to the left, creating a circle; the left-hand needle will be called Needle 1. Leave the right-hand needle (Needle 2) hanging loose. Now holding Needle 1 and slipknot in your right hand, hold cable of needle and working yarn in your left hand, with ball end of yarn going from back to front over your index finger. *Bring tip of Needle 1 toward you, under cable, then in between cable and working yarn, then over working yarn, and back under needle to the front, drawing up a loop on Needle 1; bring Needle 1 behind working yarn to create a yarnover; this is the first pair of cast-on sts. Repeat from *, casting on 2 sts at a time, until you have the required number of sts. Only count sts on the top needle, not on the cable. To begin the first round, bring Needle 2 into position to knit. You will now have two circles; if one circle is larger than the other, pull both cables to even out the circles. There should be only one twist in the needles, at the very end where Needle 1 crosses the cable (or where the cable crosses Needle 1); make sure that the two circles run parallel to each other from Needle 2 to the twist at the end. Slide the sts to the tip of Needle 2, place a marker on

Needle 1, and begin knitting. Each full round is comprised of two rings. You will have completed the first ring when you reach the st marker and it is on the cable; you will have completed the second ring (and one full round) when the st marker is on Needle 2. On the first time you work the first ring, each st will have a different orientation on the needle (leading leg in front of or behind the needle) than the following st. Each st forms a triangle between the needle and the cable below; knit into the center of the triangle. On the second ring of the first full round, you will be knitting into purled sts; this is correct.

CROCHET CHAIN

Make a slip knot and place it on crochet hook. Holding tail end of yarn in left hand, *take hook under ball end of yarn from front to back; draw yarn on hook back through previous st on hook to form new st. Repeat from * to desired number of sts or length of chain.

I-CORD

Using a double-pointed needle, cast on or pick up the required number of sts; the working yarn will be at the left-hand side of the needle. *Transfer the needle with the sts to your left hand, bring the yarn around behind the work to the right-hand side; using a second double-pointed needle, knit the sts from right to left, pulling the yarn from left to right for the first st; do not turn. Slide the sts to the opposite end of the needle; repeat from * until the I-Cord is the length desired. Note: After a few rows, the tubular shape will become apparent.

KITCHENER STITCH

Using a blunt tapestry needle, thread a length of yarn approximately 4 times the length of the section to be joined. Hold the pieces to be joined wrong sides together, with the needles holding the sts parallel, both ends pointing to the right. Working from right to left, insert tapestry needle into first st on front needle as if to purl, pull yarn through, leaving st on needle; insert tapestry needle into first st on back needle as if to knit, pull yarn through, leaving st on needle; *insert tapestry needle into first st on front needle as if to knit, pull yarn through, remove st from needle; insert tapestry needle into next st on front needle as if to purl, pull yarn through, leave st on needle; insert tapestry needle into first st on back needle as if to purl, pull yarn through, remove st from needle; insert tapestry needle into next st on back needle as if to knit, pull yarn through, leave st on needle. Repeat from *, working 3 or 4 sts at a time, then go back and adjust tension to match the pieces being joined. When 1 st remains on each needle, cut yarn and pass through last 2 sts to fasten off.

LONG-TAIL CO

Leaving tail with about 1" (2.5 cm) of yarn for each st to be cast-on, make a slipknot in the yarn and place it on the right-hand needle, with the tail to the front and the working end to the back. Insert the thumb and forefinger of your left hand between the strands of yarn so that the working end is around your forefinger and the tail end is around your thumb "slingshot" fashion; *insert the tip of the right-hand needle into the front loop on the thumb, hook the strand of yarn coming from the forefinger from back to front, and draw it through the loop on your thumb; remove your thumb from the loop and pull on the working yarn to tighten the new st on the right-hand needle; return your thumb and forefinger to their original positions, and repeat from * for remaining sts to be CO.

PROVISIONAL (CROCHET CHAIN) CO

Using a crochet hook and smooth yarn (crochet cotton or ravel cord used for machine knitting), work a crochet chain with a few more chains than the number of sts needed; fasten off. If desired, tie a knot on the fastened-off end to mark the end that you will be unraveling from later. Turn the chain over; with a needle 1 size smaller than required for piece and working yarn, starting a few chains in from the beginning of the chain, pick up and knit one st in each bump at the back of the chain, leaving any extra chains at the end unworked.

Change to needle size required for project on first row. When ready to work the live sts, unravel the chain by loosening the fastened-off end and "unzipping" the chain, placing the live sts on a spare needle.

SHORT ROW SHAPING

Work the number of sts specified in the instructions, wrap and turn (wrp-t) as follows:

To wrap a knit st, bring yarn to the front (purl position), slip the next st purlwise to the right-hand needle, bring yarn to the back of work, return the slipped st on the right-hand needle to the left-hand needle purlwise; turn, ready to work the next row, leaving the remaining sts unworked. To wrap a purl st, work as for wrapping a knit st, but bring yarn to the back (knit position) before slipping the st, and to the front after slipping the st.

When short rows are completed, or when working progressively longer short rows, work the wrap together with the wrapped st as you come to it as follows: If st is to be worked as a knit st, insert the right-hand needle into the wrap, from below, then into the wrapped st; k2tog; if st to be worked is a purl st, insert needle into the wrapped st, then down into the wrap; p2tog. (Wrap may be lifted onto the left-hand needle, then worked together with the wrapped st if this is easier.)

THREE-NEEDLE BO

Place the sts to be joined onto two same-size needles; hold the pieces to be joined with the right sides facing each other and the needles parallel, both pointing to the right. Holding both needles in your left hand, using working yarn and a third needle same size or one size larger, insert third needle into first st on front needle, then into first st on back needle; knit these two sts together; *knit next st from each needle together (two sts on right-hand needle); pass first st over second st to BO one st. Repeat from * until one st remains on third needle; cut yarn and fasten off.

ACKNOWLEDGMENTS

Thank you, first and foremost, to the woman who taught me to knit, my nana Irene Rose. While I channel your sense of humor, style, and work ethic every day, no one will ever be more dazzling than you. Mom and Dad, thank you for showing me that a life spent cultivating beauty is a life well spent.

To the women who convinced me I could make this a career, thank you. The amazing team at Webs gave me the confidence to join the Berroco design team, and I will always treasure the time spent with everyone there, especially Norah Gaughan, who I am very happy to call my yarn guru and friend.

Thank you to my speedy and competent sample knitters: Erin Birnel, Joe Green, Lara Schmidt, and Jodi Roush. Thank you to my coworkers at Skacel Collection Inc. for being tirelessly fun and inspiring.

While most of the garments in this book were knit in fervent solitude, they came alive on set with the expertise of makeup artist Erin Skipley, stylist Emilie Maslow, and her able assistant Lauren Schugar. Whether I referenced Nick Cave or beta fish, Biba Girls or August Sander, they were right there with me, ready to elevate the stunning natural beauty of my friends and models Wendy Moss, Dianna Potter, Kathlyn Rankin, Lara Schmidt, Tessa Schultz, and Kathleen Tarrant. Special thanks to Seattle Parks and Recreation and Michele and Ryan Tansey of Homestead Seattle for lending their fabulous locations, homes, and support.

The photo team was led by photographer and yarn impresario Jared Flood, with the steadfast assistance of Kathy Cadigan and Josh Green. Like many knitters, I've long admired Jared's eye and his reverence for wool and the beauty in candid moments and beloved city streets. It was incredible to have this talented Pacific Northwest native involved. I spent a week showing him my work and my Seattle, and I am thrilled to call him a colleague and a friend.

Thank you to the companies who graciously provided yarn and notions: Berroco Inc., Cascade Yarns Inc., Fairmount Fibers Ltd., JHB International, Kelbourne Woolens, Tunney Wool, Madelinetosh, Neighborhood Fiber Co., One World Button Supply Co., Peace Fleece, Zealana, and Skacel Collection Inc. Find detailed information about these companies in Sources for Supplies on page 139. The fibers and notions I chose are each outstanding in their own way, and I encourage you to seek them out.

My heartfelt thanks to my hard-working and talented friends who have supported and inspired me throughout this process: Richard and Sarah Bianculli, Josh Bennett, Olga Buraya-Kefelian, Ragnheiður Eiríksdóttir, Kate Gagnon-Osborn, Elliott Gray, Chelsea Gunn, Gudrun Johnston, Jimad Khan, Courtney Kelley, Lee Meredith, Mary Jane Mucklestone, Clara Parkes, Matthew Lidfors Robinson, Jessica Rose-Kim, Andrea Rangel, Ysolda Teague, Stephen West, and Jenna Wilbur. Thank you to the knitters I haven't met who have knit my patterns or sent me a kind word—I truly appreciate it.

Deepest thanks to my tech editors, Sue McCain and Robin Melanson, for molding my scattered thoughts into clear, knittable patterns, and making it a learning process rather than a chore. Tremendous thanks are due to my editor, Melanie Falick. Your books inspired me before I even knew I was a knitwear designer! Thank you for your patience and guidance through this process. I'm honored to be a part of your inimitable body of work.

ABOUT THE AUTHOR

KATHY CADIGAN

Cirilia Rose's citizenship in the yarn industry was quite accidental. While studying consumer culture and aesthetics in western Massachusetts, she took a job at her local yarn store that just happened to be one of the largest in the country. Since then she has gone on to teach, write, style, produce, and design in conjunction with a wide variety of industry leaders from Berroco Inc. and Skacel Collection Inc. to *Vogue Knitting*, from Creativebug to Brooklyn Tweed.

As an undergraduate she developed and taught a colloquium on the decline of originality in popular culture. She continued this inquiry in graduate school, examining how people use clothing and objects to construct and perform identity, delving into the world of advertising, fashion, and art. As her crafting life expanded, she became interested in the friction between feminism and domesticity, and the implications of reference in art and craft, settling on bricolage as a way to honor the past while creating new work. While she eventually left academia for the fiber world, her studies inform her approach to product design, promotion, and craft.

She currently works as a freelance designer and consultant. The rest of her time is devoted to watching movies, making messes in the kitchen, and visiting far-flung friends. Her passion for knitwear fuels her every day, and she strives to share that with knitters and non-knitters alike.